sf
Service
Discipline
Relationships
Honesty
Integrity
Prudence
Fair play
THE
SUNDARAM
WAY
Humility
Openness

THE ALTERNATES UNIVERSE

Exploring the World of Alternative Investments

An initiative by

Contents

▶ Contents ◀

Preface by Sundaram Alternates

At Sundaram Alternates, we are committed to providing investors with tailored financial solutions that address their individual needs. Being a wholly-owned subsidiary of Sundaram Asset Management Company (SAMC) and a part of the prestigious Sundaram Finance Group, we have established a solid reputation in Portfolio Management Services (PMS) and Alternative Investment Funds (AIF). Our goal is simple yet ambitious: we strive to assist investors in creating long-term wealth through creative methods that combine growth and safety. Our skilled team focuses on areas such as private credit and equities to achieve returns that are both optimized and considerate of risk. By having a thorough knowledge of market trends, we discover opportunities that may be overlooked by others.

We strongly believe in ethical leadership and making purposeful investments. By incorporating Environmental, Social, and Governance (ESG) principles in our strategies, we protect our clients' assets and make a positive impact on our shared world. Sundaram Alternates continues to lead India's asset management industry as a pioneer in alternative investments. Our vision is to continue developing as a vibrant and inventive company, remaining loyal to the principles that have influenced us throughout our history. In this book, The Alternates Universe, we feature conversations with CEOs and CXOs from a range of industries. These discussions cover the trends, challenges, and the future of finance, along with the role alternate investments will play. Each chapter distills key insights from these dialogs, offering perspectives from leaders who, like us, are focused on pushing boundaries and creating long-term value.

We welcome you to explore and benefit from the wealth of knowledge being shared in this book as we work toward molding the future of alternative investments in India.

Preface by PMS Bazaar

The investment landscape is rapidly evolving, prompting investors to seek effective strategies to navigate its complexities. In response, we collaborated with the Sundaram Alternates team to launch **The Alternates Universe**, an informative webinar series featuring leading figures from the investment industry.

The first season was a remarkable success, drawing over 6,700 registrations across 12 episodes. This book aims to compile and present the invaluable insights shared by our esteemed speakers during the webinars. We take pride in partnering with Sundaram Alternates on this initiative, guided by Vikaas M Sachdeva, Managing Director of Sundaram Alternates, whose leadership was crucial to this project's success.

Our mission is straightforward yet ambitious: to make essential insights more accessible to a broader audience. Featuring perspectives from 12 renowned experts, this book offers a unique opportunity to gain a comprehensive understanding of alternative investments, serving as a valuable resource for sophisticated investors.

Rather than focusing on a single topic, this book explores various aspects of the alternative investment landscape, including diverse product offerings, the importance of asset allocation, the role of technology in wealth management, global wealth creation trends, expert analyses of equity and debt markets, and macroeconomic factors influencing investments. Readers will uncover insights that are often difficult to find elsewhere.

The featured experts share practical strategies and reflections, providing lessons grounded in real-world experience. Their discussions offer actionable approaches for navigating today's markets and adapting to global economic shifts.

At PMS Bazaar, our mission is to transform the investment landscape. With over 73,000 subscribers, we provide unmatched access to diverse Portfolio Management Services (PMS) and Alternative Investment Funds (AIFs). We hope The Alternates Universe serves as a valuable resource for navigating wealth creation complexities, offering strategic guidance and insights into the future of investments.

Exploring The Alternates Universe: The World of Alternative Investments

The Alternates Universe webinar series is a groundbreaking initiative by Sundaram Alternates, a pioneer in the PMS and AIF sector. This series goes beyond traditional asset management discussions by inviting influential leaders and CEOs to share their perspectives. Through engaging interactions, we delve into the minds of those managing HNI clients and wealth managers, uncovering valuable insights and innovative strategies. The name "**The Alternates Universe**" was chosen to capture the boundless and diverse opportunities within alternative investments, much like navigating a new and unexplored universe filled with potential and promise.

Presented by the Sundaram Learning and Information Center, The Alternates Universe webinar series highlights Sundaram Alternates' commitment to advancing discussions and driving innovation in the alternative investments sector. Partnering as the platform host, PMS Bazaar ensures these discussions reach a wider audience. Spearheading this initiative is Mr. Vikaas M Sachdeva, an industry stalwart with over three decades of experience in the asset management business. As the Managing Director of Sundaram Alternates, Vikaas drives growth across various platforms, geographies, and asset classes. He has the unique distinction of having been at the cusp of the growth and evolution of the asset management and alternatives industries, playing a key role in their pivotal expansion. His illustrious career includes pivotal roles at leading financial service organizations, where he has been instrumental in turning around businesses and driving innovation.

Vikaas's extensive expertise spans global and domestic sales, investment management, digital and physical distribution, marketing, HR, and customer service. His industry affiliations include serving on the AMFI board, co-chairing the Indian Venture and Alternate Capital Association (IVCA) and the Indian FinTech Forum, and being a member of a plant-based advisory firm.

The Alternates Universe series features engaging conversations between Vikaas, his co-hosts, and various esteemed guests, delving deep into the intricacies of asset management, investment strategies, and market trends. Each episode offers a wealth of knowledge, making it essential for investors seeking to stay ahead in the financial world.

Foreword by Mr. Harsha Viji
Executive Vice Chairman, Sundaram Finance Limited

For nearly seven decades, the Sundaram Finance Group has stood for integrity, prudence, and service in the financial services sector. Since our beginnings in 1954, Sundaram Finance has grown into a multifaceted financial conglomerate, deeply rooted in its values and guided by a vision to provide consistent, thoughtful leadership in an ever-changing world. Across our diverse businesses, including Mutual Funds, Housing Finance, Insurance, and Alternate Assets, we have continued to build on this foundation of trust. At Sundaram Alternate Assets, a subsidiary of Sundaram Asset Management, we pride ourselves on our forward-looking approach and commitment to innovation. Over the years, we have successfully handled the complexities of the alternate investment space, combining our legacy of prudence with a modern, dynamic outlook.

In keeping with this spirit of innovation, The Alternates Universe webinar series was conceived as a platform to explore new dimensions of thought leadership in the PMS and AIF sectors. The series has provided a rare opportunity for industry leaders and CEOs to engage in meaningful discussions, offering their insights on the evolving nature of alternative investments. These conversations have offered unique perspectives on the challenges and opportunities faced by those managing wealth for High-Net-Worth-Individuals (HNIs). What started as a series of engaging dialogs has now been thoughtfully compiled into this book, capturing the essence of these discussions for a broader audience. Through this book, readers are invited to explore new ideas, strategies, and insights that go beyond traditional asset management. It showcases Sundaram's unwavering commitment to providing innovative solutions while staying true to the values that have been the foundation of our growth.

I believe The Alternates Universe will serve as a valuable resource for professionals and investors alike, offering fresh perspectives and guiding us through the complexities of the financial world. I am honored to be part of this journey and confident that the insights captured here will continue to contribute meaningfully to the discourse in our industry.

Warm regards,

Harsha Viji

Foreword by Mr. Vikaas M Sachdeva
Managing Director, Sundaram Alternate Assets Ltd.

When I joined Sundaram Alternates as Managing Director, it was clear that the potential for growth in this industry was immense. Our focus has always been on building strategies that go beyond the conventional, bringing fresh ideas and value to our clients across different markets and asset classes. I've been fortunate to have a career that has allowed me to work with and lead some of the most dynamic financial institutions, from starting my journey with Birla Sun Life International AMC Ltd. to steering Edelweiss Asset Management and Enam Asset Management through transformative phases. Each step has been a lesson in what it takes to stay ahead in a competitive environment—by challenging norms and exploring new avenues.

When The Alternates Universe series came into the picture, I realized it was unique. It isn't merely a typical forum for conversation; it's a platform that truly brings together individuals, ideas, and viewpoints in a meaningful manner. One standout aspect for me has been its ability to present challenging topics, such as alternative investments, in a way that piques interest and encourages involvement. It brings out real-world applications and thought-provoking insights, making it incredibly valuable for wealth managers and investors alike. One of the most impactful moments for me during the series was when we discussed the role of alternate investments in bringing stability amidst market fluctuations. It struck a chord because it mirrors the shifts I've seen throughout my career. The way this series explores these aspects helps break down barriers and build a deeper understanding of strategies that go beyond the traditional.

As we look ahead to the next season, I'd love to see more focus on how technology is influencing our space and what new investment themes are on the horizon. There is a lot more to discover, and I believe the series will continue to push limits. To all the readers starting this book, I hope you enjoy it as much as I did when I was involved in the series. There is a wealth of information on these pages, and I believe it will offer you fresh viewpoints that challenge your current thoughts on investments. Wishing the team ongoing success, I'm excited to see where the journey will lead us next!

Warm regards,

Vikaas M Sachdeva

Chapter 01

Strategic Approaches for the Modern Investor[1]

- This chapter delves into the intricacies of contemporary investment strategies and examines the impact of global trends on reshaping the investment sector.

- Guest Speaker: Mr. Satheesh Krishnamurthy*, Executive Vice President & Head Private, Premium and Third-party Products, Axis Bank.

  Mr. Satheesh Krishnamurthy is a seasoned thought leader with over two decades of experience in the financial services sector. He has held pivotal roles in premier banking institutions, pioneering innovative wealth management solutions. His notable achievements include the launch of Axis Bank's premium brand, Burgundy, and driving significant growth in assets under management, positioning him as a key figure in the industry.

- Speaker: Mr. Madanagopal Ramu, Head of Equity and Fund Manager, Sundaram Alternate Assets Ltd.

  With over 18 years of experience in the Indian Financial Markets, Mr. Madanagopal Ramu currently manages Assets Under Management (AUM) of around Rs. 3500 crores and has over 8 years of experience in managing funds. He manages

---

1   This chapter is based on The Alternates Universe episode shot on 20-01-23.

*   The speaker has transitioned to a leadership role at a private wealth firm.

Sundaram India Secular Opportunities Portfolio (SISOP), Sundaram Emerging Leadership Fund (S.E.L.F.) and Voyager PMS strategies, which have won awards at PMS Bazaar's PMS Rankings FY 21-22 event.

The Person Behind the Professional

Behind Mr. Satheesh Krishnamurthy's professional demeanor lies a persona that intrigues those who interact with him. Colleagues not only admire but actively engage with him, noting particular quirks that define his personality. Described as a stickler for punctuality, Mr. Krishnamurthy ensures that agendas are adhered to with precision, demonstrating a firm aversion to inefficiency. Despite maintaining a composed exterior reminiscent of the cricketing legend Dhoni, his body language subtly betrays his true sentiments, according to those acquainted with him.

A voracious reader, Mr. Krishnamurthy reads a book weekly, showcasing a keen intellect and a remarkable memory that allows him to recollect passages from texts read years prior. With a penchant for the works of P.G. Wodehouse, an avid interest in cricket, and a history as a competitive chess player, his diverse interests add depth to his character.

Notably, regardless of his global travels, he steadfastly seeks out Indian cuisine, particularly favoring dal and rice, a testament to his culinary preferences. Renowned for his wit, Mr. Krishnamurthy's humor shines through, as exemplified by a memorable response during a Citibank interview, where he quipped about the track record of those who hired him. Such anecdotes illustrate his quick wit and self-assured conduct.

Introduction

Today's investment strategies are getting more complex, mixing traditional methods with new techniques to navigate the twists and turns of the financial world. Investors are using a mix of smart asset allocation, momentum investing, and dollar-cost averaging to boost returns and handle risks. The rise of things like private equity and real estate is changing how portfolios look, and tech tools like automated trading systems and blockchain are making decisions smarter. Also, the focus on sustainable and ethical investing is all about lining up financial goals with personal values. These strategies keep evolving with global economic changes and world events, so investors need to stay flexible and well-informed to seize opportunities and manage risks effectively.

India's Position in Global Investments

India has really stepped up its game in global investments, drawing in a lot of foreign cash and venture capital thanks to its strong economic growth and investor-friendly environment. In 2022, India snagged the fourth spot worldwide in tech investments, raking in a cool $24.1 billion and showing off its booming tech industry. Initiatives like "Make in India" and loosening up on foreign investment rules have made India a hot spot for international money. Also, economic changes like the Goods and Services Tax (GST) and setting up Special Economic Zones (SEZs) have brought more clarity and tax perks, boosting investors' trust. And with a growing middle class and folks having more money to spend, India's domestic market is full of chances to grow, making it a key player for investments globally right now.

Vikaas M Sachdeva: My first question to you is, as Indians, we tend to think that India is the center of the universe for every investor. However, does an evolved investor with a global perspective view India as an investment destination with the same intensity as they would from their country's perspective?

Satheesh Krishnamurthy: The questions around India and, how investors are pursuing India, and how we, as Indians, obviously look at India as the center of the universe are very interesting. If one ever had to think about India as the center of the universe, it is now. So, it is a good spot to be in, in more ways than one. In fact, I was looking at some data as well. If you look at how foreign investors are looking at India, very clearly when they look at India, they see a very strong economy. We have broken the rest of the pack in the way our markets performed in 2022. It shows resilience in our economy very clearly. The stability of the government is an important factor. You look at the reforms that are being undertaken, and they are set up fairly well. So, India is getting even more diplomatic muscle. We also have the presidency of the G20, as we all know. So, very clearly, there is a lot of overarching, let's call it, the realization of India's both hard power and soft power coming into play.

Now, how is that playing out in the world of investments? When I look at how India was bucketed among emerging markets in the past, India was a subset of emerging markets in most indexes, and China used to have a dedicated allocation. Now, when we look at the MSCI Emerging Markets index, India has almost doubled its weight. So, that's a clear indication of India's growing muscle. You look at China. On the other hand, its weightage has fallen for the first time below 27. So, we are clearly fairly behind China, but notwithstanding that, given the way we are a democracy, we have our own pace of growth by getting everybody along. India is turning a corner there. There is also a very clear shift in the way foreign portfolio investors are looking at China within their basket of emerging markets. Everybody is talking about China plus one. So, their focus is also becoming, in a way, diversified out of China. And, of course, other markets, like Korea and Taiwan, are benefiting from this change, too. The other factor that is working very clearly for India is the equity cult, which is gaining ground again. When I looked at the data, 4.8 percent of Indian household assets as of March 22 are in equities, and this was about 4.3. So, a 50-basis point increase in a year is not a bad deal at all. If you were to look back even as recently as 2020, that number was 2.7 percent. So, very clearly, we did see that all through the COVID phase, loads of Demat accounts were getting opened, and more and more customers were entering into this equity cult. So, I think that India is very important overall.

At the same time, when you look at the Ultra HNIs and the HNI segment of customers, they look at global investing. India is obviously their home ground, but they also want to diversify from a currency standpoint and a geography standpoint and gain alpha by investing in markets that may have been battered over the last year or so. So, there are opportunities emerging. I would also state that for Ultra HNIs, I find that the variable capital company or VCC structure in Singapore, known for several collective investment schemes, whether open or closed-ended, may pool funds for investment purposes. Simultaneously, this structure ensures that individual client assets are segregated from each other. These are aspects that I find are gaining ground subsequently.

Profile of HNIs and Ultra HNIs

High-Net-Worth-Individuals (HNIs) and Ultra-High-Net-Worth-Individuals (Ultra HNIs) hold significant positions in the financial world because of their substantial investable assets. In India, HNIs are individuals with investable assets over Rs 5 crore, while Ultra HNIs have assets exceeding Rs 25 crore. These individuals typically include business owners, corporate executives, and entrepreneurs, and they play a crucial role in the economy, collectively possessing wealth worth nearly $1.5 trillion, which accounts for about 58% of India's GDP. They have varied investment preferences, such as real estate, stocks, and alternative assets like sovereign gold bonds and hedged equity products.

Vikaas M Sachdeva: Typically, when you talk about an HNI or Ultra HNI, what comes to mind is someone who's very senior, 60 plus, looking at some very conventional investment avenues. But with the changing economic and business fields, has the demographic profile of a typical Ultra HNI or HNI evolved? What's your view?

Satheesh Krishnamurthy: I think it's a great question because we are clearly a generation living through multiple inflection points. One such inflection point is how the past picture of an Ultra HNI being a late 50s person who's really been a businessman and who's had to slog through multiple decades to get there is changing quite radically. The first clear trend I see is that cities in tier 2 and tier 3 now account for 50 percent of recognized startups in India. Wealth is getting created from these cities. For example, the startup base in Tenkasi is creating waves.

Another trend is that in metropolitan cities, there is a degree of saturation from a cost and availability of infrastructure standpoint. In this work-from-anywhere model, entrepreneurs are thinking beyond geographical boundaries. Another impact is the increasing number of multinational companies setting up shop across locations in India. According to a management consultancy report, about 976 multinational companies have set up 1257 global in-house centers in India. This indicates that India is emerging as a hub for multinational companies globally.

Additionally, the startup community is attracting a lot of funding, with financing for startups in tier 2 and tier 3 cities up by 15 percent. Tier 2 startups in India raised over a billion dollars across some 300 deals. The mutual fund industry's popularity is also expanding beyond the top 30 geographical locations. Clearly, the profile of Ultra HNIs is changing. Entrepreneurs, some barely in their 20s or even high teens, are willing to take risks and experiment across various industries. Tech is a unifying theme for scale. That's the way I see this.

Trends in the Banking Sector

In 2024, the banking sector is gearing up for some big changes driven by key trends. Digital transformation is a top priority, as banks are pouring resources into AI, cloud tech, and digital identities to improve how customers are served and how operations run smoothly. Regulations are still a big deal, pushing for solid compliance and risk management plans. Economic factors like fluctuating interest rates and inflation bring both hurdles and chances, affecting profits and costs. Work expectations are changing, too, calling for a mix of remote work and face-to-face teamwork. Advisory services are making a comeback, and sustainable finance is in the spotlight due to market demands and rules. Despite the challenges, the future looks bright, with room to grow through tech upgrades and smart innovation.

Vikaas M Sachdeva: Could you elaborate on the trends you're observing in the banking sector and their implications?

Satheesh Krishnamurthy: Certainly! The banking sector is undergoing a significant transformation driven by factors such as consolidation, improved balance sheets, and digital innovation. One notable trend is the consolidation among banks, with larger institutions gaining market share. This trend has positive implications for the sector's stability and efficiency, as it allows for better risk management and economies of scale.

Additionally, there has been a marked improvement in corporate NPA cycles, indicating a healthier lending environment. The digitization of banking processes has also been a game-changer, revolutionizing everything from underwriting to payments. This digital transformation not only enhances operational efficiency but also opens up new avenues for revenue generation and customer engagement.

Looking ahead, we believe that the banking sector will continue to play a crucial role in driving economic growth, particularly through increased lending to key sectors such as manufacturing and retail. With India's credit-to-GDP ratio still below that of developed economies, there remains ample room for growth in retail credit, which is poised to benefit from rising consumption and improving economic sentiment.

Real Estate Investment Vehicles

Real estate investment options provide a range of chances for investors to join the real estate market, each with its own perks. Common choices include Real Estate Investment Trusts (REITs), real estate private equity (REPE), and real estate operating companies (REOCs). REITs are like publicly traded companies that handle income-generating properties and give out most of their earnings as dividends, giving you a mix of liquidity and regular income. REPE involves combining funds from wealthy investors to buy and manage real estate assets, often aiming for value growth and offering tax benefits, but with more risk and less flexibility to pull out funds. REOCs work much like REITs but allow more freedom in investment strategies and payment plans, even though they may not be as tax-efficient. Each option suits different types of investors, risk preferences, and investment objectives, so it's important for investors to match their selections with their financial goals and timelines.

Vikaas M Sachdeva: Shifting our focus to real estate, how do you perceive the evolving situation, especially with the emergence of alternative investment vehicles like real estate debt and REITs?

Satheesh Krishnamurthy: Real estate continues to be a cornerstone of investment portfolios, offering diversification and potential for attractive returns. However, the traditional approach to real estate investment is evolving with the emergence of alternative vehicles such as real estate debt instruments and REITs.

One notable development is the growing popularity of REITs, which provide investors with access to grade-A commercial properties while offering liquidity and transparency. This trend is reshaping the real estate business, as it allows investors to gain exposure to the sector without the complexities of direct ownership.

Similarly, real estate debt instruments are gaining traction as an alternative investment avenue, offering fixed income returns with lower volatility compared to equity investments. These instruments provide investors with the opportunity to participate in real estate markets while mitigating risks associated with property ownership.

Overall, the emergence of alternative investment vehicles in the real estate sector is democratizing access to this asset class and providing investors with greater flexibility and diversification opportunities.

Role of GIFT City in Global Investments

Gujarat International Finance Tec-City (GIFT City) is a key player in global investments, providing a top-notch financial and tech hub in India. Being India's first International Financial Services Center (IFSC), GIFT City sets the stage with world-class regulations, tax perks, and streamlined processes, drawing in investors from near and far. It caters to a variety of financial activities like banking, insurance, and capital markets, offering notable tax benefits and exemptions. By attracting global investors and corps, GIFT City not only boosts India's financial sector but also elevates India's economic status on the world stage.

Vikaas M Sachdeva: Lastly, let's touch upon the ever-changing alternative asset classes and the role of platforms like GIFT City in facilitating global investments.

Satheesh Krishnamurthy: GIFT City represents a significant opportunity for investors seeking to diversify their portfolios and access global markets. By providing a conducive regulatory environment and attractive tax incentives, GIFT City enables investors to explore a wide range of investment opportunities across asset classes.

One prominent trend is the growing interest in alternative asset classes such as Venture Capital, Private Equity, and hedge funds, which offer higher returns and portfolio diversification. Platforms like GIFT City play a crucial role in facilitating investments in these asset classes by providing a streamlined process and access to global markets.

Furthermore, GIFT City serves as a gateway for foreign investors looking to invest in India, offering a transparent and efficient platform for capital deployment. As GIFT City continues to evolve, we expect to see increased participation from both domestic and international investors, driving innovation and growth in India's financial markets.

Key Takeaways

- **India's Rising Investment Appeal:** India's strong economic performance, stable government, and growing diplomatic influence are increasingly attracting foreign investors. The country's elevated position in the MSCI Emerging Markets index and the growing domestic interest in equity investments highlight its expanding role in the global investment sector.

- **Changing Wealth Demographics:** The profile of High-Net-Worth-Individuals (HNWIs) and Ultra-High-Net-Worth-Individuals (Ultra HNWIs) is evolving, with wealth creation spreading beyond traditional urban centers and older demographics to include younger entrepreneurs and residents of smaller cities.

- **Banking Sector Developments:** The banking sector is experiencing significant changes driven by consolidation, improved balance sheets, and advancements in digital technology. These trends are contributing to increased stability and operational efficiency.

- **Growth of Alternative Investments:** Real Estate Investment Trusts (REITs) and real estate debt instruments are gaining traction as flexible investment options that provide diversification and potential returns.

- **GIFT City's Strategic Role:** GIFT City is becoming a key player in global investments by offering a favorable regulatory environment and tax benefits, facilitating easier global investments and providing opportunities for portfolio diversification.

Chapter 02

NRI Insights: Private Markets & Diverse Assets[2]

- This chapter discusses how NRIs can manage their investments, understand tax implications, and leverage fintech solutions to optimize their portfolios more effectively.

- Guest Speaker: Mr. Krishnan Ramachandran, CEO, Barjeel Geojit Financial Services.

  Mr. Krishnan Ramachandran, a chartered accountant, has over 30 years of experience in financial services. He has been the CEO of Barjeel Geojit Financial Services LLC in Dubai since 2006 and oversees various GCC joint ventures of Geojit Financial Services Limited.

- Speaker: Mr. Ajit Narasimhan, Chief Marketing Officer, Sundaram Asset Management Company.

  Mr. Ajit Narasimhan has over 19 years of experience leading high-performing Business Development and Product Management teams in Mutual Funds and FinTech. He has held roles across Investment Products, Marketing, and Digital Business, playing a key role in Sundaram Mutual's digital transformation and the development of its digi-retail strategy. Under his leadership, the brand has achieved significant growth on various digital platforms.

---

2   This chapter is based on The Alternates Universe episode shot on 03-03-23.

- Speaker: Mr. Madanagopal Ramu, Head of Equity Fund Management, Sundaram Alternates.

With over 18 years of experience in the Indian Financial Markets, Mr. Madanagopal Ramu currently manages Assets Under Management (AUM) of around Rs. 3500 crores and has over 8 years of experience in managing funds. He manages Sundaram India Secular Opportunities Portfolio (SISOP), Sundaram Emerging Leadership Fund (S.E.L.F.) and Voyager PMS strategies, which have won awards at PMS Bazaar's PMS Rankings FY 21-22 event.

Foreword

In my role as the CEO of Barjeel Geojit Financial Services LLC, I have had the opportunity to navigate the financial industry for more than 30 years, with a focus on wealth management, private equity, and corporate finance. During my 18 years at Barjeel Geojit, we have consistently worked to present India as an attractive investment option for NRIs in the UAE. Our company has cemented its position as a top financial intermediary in the UAE and is committed to equipping investors with the necessary resources and understanding to efficiently handle their finances. Our goal is to offer customized financial solutions that meet our clients' varied needs and build trust and transparency.

The Alternates Universe series plays a vital role in wealth management and alternative investments. It illuminates changes in investor preferences and the growth of alternative investments like private equity, real estate, hedge funds, and commodities. This program emphasizes the crucial move towards varied portfolios, highlighting the role of alternatives in risk management and attaining greater returns. What really strikes a chord with me is the focus of the series on giving people access to high-quality financial education and insights, mirroring our commitment at Barjeel Geojit to empower our clients with knowledge and well-informed choices.

Being part of this series gave me the opportunity to discuss how the viewpoint on options has evolved over time, especially for Non-Resident Indians (NRIs). There is an increasing awareness of the importance of using alternatives for diversification and managing volatility, particularly in today's unpredictable global markets. Upon reflecting on my experiences, I realized the importance of structured investing and risk management in our discussions.

It strengthened my conviction in the importance of a structured investment strategy, particularly in a volatile market. This viewpoint is crucial for investors looking to maneuver through the intricacies of both conventional and unconventional investments.

The Alternates Universe offers a thorough perspective on the alternative investment industry, giving valuable information on the different asset classes and strategies that characterize this field. It discusses the possibilities and difficulties encountered by both investors and fund managers, serving as an essential tool for those seeking to enhance their knowledge of alternative investments. The series is a valuable platform for wealth managers to share best practices and explore new approaches to investment strategy and portfolio management. For investors, it provides a guide to grasping the possibilities of alternative investments and incorporating them into an overall investment plan for increased profits and risk management.

I am optimistic about the possibility of The Alternates Universe continuing to facilitate meaningful conversations and encouraging cooperation among industry experts as we move forward. I am interested in seeing more emphasis on the use of technology to enhance investment strategies and improve client experiences in the upcoming season. Readers are encouraged to make use of the abundant knowledge this book offers. It provides a special chance to enhance one's comprehension of the alternative investment industry and to be proactive in a constantly evolving financial environment.

Thank you to the team behind The Alternates Universe for creating this platform and for their dedication to advancing the knowledge and practice of wealth management.

The Person Behind the Professional

Renowned for his integrity and honesty, Mr. Krishnan exudes authenticity in every aspect of his life. A devoted family man, he finds solace and joy in the company of his beloved wife and two daughters, each a source of pride and inspiration. With a penchant for exploration, Mr. Krishnan cherishes destinations like Switzerland and Paris. An enthusiast for the finer things in life, Mr. Krishnan shares a passion for automobiles, particularly favoring the Hyundai brand. His love for cinema knows no bounds, with a keen eye for the latest Tamil and Malayalam releases, a passion that resonates with peers both near and far. A polyglot with fluency in multiple languages, including Hindi, Krishnan's linguistic prowess helped build a vast network of connections, enriching both his personal and professional spheres.

Beyond his personal interests, Mr. Krishnan remains abreast of technological advancements, eagerly embracing the latest gadgets and trends. However, it is in his professional domain where Krishnan truly shines, revered for his unwavering commitment to customer satisfaction and a resolute customer-centric ethos. Despite his amiable demeanor, Krishnan harbors disdain for fruitless arguments devoid of solutions, a testament to his pragmatism and efficiency. Yet, amidst his myriad qualities, Krishnan's journey is one of continual self-improvement, exemplified by his ongoing endeavor to overcome challenges such as smoking cessation.

Introduction

For Non-Resident Indians (NRIs), private markets and alternative investments offer intriguing opportunities to diversify their portfolios beyond traditional stocks and bonds. These investments, which include private equity, real estate, hedge funds, and commodities, can provide higher returns and less correlation with public markets, making them attractive for those looking to enhance their investment strategy. However, NRIs must navigate various regulatory and tax considerations when investing in these markets, as rules can differ significantly from those in their country of residence. Additionally, the illiquid nature of many alternative investments means NRIs should carefully assess their risk tolerance and investment horizon. Despite these challenges, the potential for substantial returns, coupled with the ability to invest in emerging sectors and innovative companies, makes private markets and alternative investments a compelling option for NRIs seeking to broaden their financial horizons.

Changes in Alternatives for NRIs

The perception of alternative investments has shifted drastically. Once reserved for institutions and high-net-worth-individuals, they've now entered the mainstream. Investors are increasingly turning to options like private equity, real estate, and hedge funds to reduce reliance on traditional stocks and bonds. The 2007-2009 financial crisis exposed the limits of conventional markets, prompting many to explore alternatives that aren't as closely tied to public market movements. Technological advancements and regulatory shifts have also made these investments more accessible. Today, alternatives are seen as valuable additions to a diversified portfolio, offering unique opportunities for enhanced risk-adjusted returns.

Ajit Narasimhan: Can you elaborate on your journey and how the perspective on Alternatives has changed over the years?

Krishnan Ramachandran: Over my 30-year tenure in the industry, I've seen significant changes, particularly in the outlook of NRIs. Initially, NRIs were viewed as non-returning Indians, but now they're more global in their investment outlook, seeking returns wherever viable. Our company, Barjeel Geojit Financial Services, has been serving NRIs in the UAE for 20 years. Initially India-centric, we've seen a shift towards global investments, reflecting NRIs' changing preferences.

Benefits and Tax Implications for NRIs

NRIs have diverse investment options in India, including equities, mutual funds, real estate, and fixed deposits. These can often deliver higher returns than developed markets. Real estate, in particular, holds strong potential due to ongoing urbanization and economic growth. Investing in India can also support retirement planning or act as a financial cushion for unforeseen events. However, NRIs need to consider tax implications carefully. Indian tax laws apply to any income earned in the country—such as long-term capital gains on listed shares taxed at 10% and short-term gains at 15%. By understanding tax liabilities and utilizing Double Taxation Avoidance Agreements (DTAAs), NRIs can reduce tax burdens and maximize returns. While the opportunities are promising, awareness of both benefits and tax obligations is key.

Ajit Narasimhan: Moving into the specifics, what are the potential benefits and tax implications for NRIs investing in Alternatives?

Krishnan Ramachandran: Alternatives have gained traction due to their compelling investment case. However, NRIs face certain disadvantages compared to domestic investors, such as limited options and complex regulatory requirements. Tax implications are also a concern, with interest income from NRE accounts being taxed at a maximum rate of 30%. Despite these challenges, Alternatives offer diversification and potentially higher returns, making them attractive to NRIs.

Impact of Global Events on NRI Investments

Global events like COVID-19 and the Russia-Ukraine war have significantly influenced NRI investment decisions. The pandemic triggered a steep drop in global GDP in 2020, with recovery efforts stabilizing markets only gradually. The Russia-Ukraine conflict, starting in 2022, added to the turmoil, pushing up inflation and disrupting commodity and energy markets. For NRIs, this volatility highlights the need for diversification and proactive risk management. Fluctuating energy prices and geopolitical instability have made it crucial to stay informed and adjust strategies as needed to protect investments and seize new opportunities in both Indian and global markets.

Madanagopal Ramu: In the last three to four years, post-COVID, a lot of money is getting pumped into the market, and then we have this Russia-Ukraine war happening. Has anything dramatically changed in the way NRIs look at the various options in front of them? Obviously, India is looking better because the economy is doing well, and people are interested in India. Is this the only reason why the economy is the only reason why NRIs are looking more at India, or are there not many options available, and that is really creating a prospect scenario for India?

Krishnan Ramachandran: Post-COVID, there has been a sea change in the interests of NRIs. Globally, investors have behaved very differently, even in India. We saw a surge in new accounts and investments during the lockdown, reflecting a serious interest in India's resilient market. However, the volatility over the past year also highlighted the importance of structured investing and risk management for NRIs. In 2022, all asset classes across the world delivered negative returns, except for commodities. This was an unpredictable event, and it's likely that NRIs will look at more structured ways of investing and global cues more seriously in the coming years.

Changes in the Advisory Space and Regulatory Requirements

The advisory space has transformed rapidly, fueled by technology and evolving regulations. Digital platforms and robo-advisors have made investment guidance more accessible and affordable, extending services to a wider audience. Enhanced data analytics now enable advisors to deliver more precise and personalized recommendations. On the regulatory side, increased focus on transparency and investor protection has led to stricter compliance standards. Rules like the fiduciary requirement in the U.S. mandate advisors to prioritize client interests and minimize conflicts of interest. As a result, advisors are adopting more rigorous processes and redefining their value propositions to stay competitive in a client-focused, ethics-driven market.

Madanagopal Ramu: Shifting the focus to the advisory space, how has it changed, and are regulatory requirements more stringent for alternatives compared to traditional investments? How do you compare the two?

Krishnan Ramachandran: The advisory space has become more crucial, with clients being better informed and having diverse needs. Financial advisors play a vital role in understanding clients' unique requirements and providing personalized advice. Regulatory oversight, especially for alternatives, has increased globally, necessitating compliance with strict norms like AML monitoring and FATCA reporting. Advisors must navigate these regulations to ensure client interests are protected.

Due Diligence Process

A thorough due diligence process is key to making informed investment decisions. Start by analyzing the fundamentals—financial health, performance, and market position of the asset or company. Evaluate industry trends and competitive positioning to gauge growth potential and risks. Review legal and regulatory compliance to spot any red flags. Assess the management team's expertise and track record for insights into operational effectiveness. Finally, ensure the investment aligns with your financial goals, risk tolerance, and time horizon. By covering these bases, investors can confidently decide if an opportunity fits within their broader portfolio strategy.

Ajit Narasimhan: Could you shed light on the due diligence process before onboarding an investment strategy for your investors?

Krishnan Ramachandran: Certainly, our due diligence process emphasizes track record, pedigree, and sustainability. We assess a strategy's performance over a significant period, looking for consistent returns and robust portfolio management. Our back-office analytics enable proactive monitoring and predictive analysis, ensuring informed investment decisions for our clients.

Leveraging Fintech Solutions

Fintech solutions are reshaping how businesses and individuals handle finances. Technologies like mobile payments, blockchain, and robo-advisors enable faster transactions, cost savings, and better data insights. Businesses can optimize operations and make smarter decisions, while individuals gain easier access to banking, investments, and lending services—all from their devices. Fintech also boosts security, offering strong safeguards for sensitive information. By embracing these innovations, businesses and individuals can stay agile and competitive in a digital-first world.

Ajit Narasimhan: How can NRIs use fintech solutions to manage their finances and investments more effectively?

Krishnan Ramachandran: NRIs can use fintech solutions to manage their finances and investments more effectively by using digital platforms, mobile apps, and online tools offered by banks, wealth management firms, and fintech startups. They can use digital banking platforms to access account information, make transactions, and track their financial activities conveniently from anywhere in the world. Mobile apps and robo-advisory platforms offer automated investment solutions based on algorithms and data analytics, providing personalized investment recommendations and portfolio management services suited to individual goals and risk profiles. Moreover, fintech solutions such as peer-to-peer lending platforms, crowdfunding platforms, and digital wealth management platforms offer alternative investment opportunities and access to diversified portfolios beyond traditional asset classes. Additionally, NRIs can use fintech solutions for currency exchange, remittance services, and cross-border payments, offering competitive exchange rates, lower fees, and faster transaction processing compared to traditional banking channels. By embracing fintech solutions, NRIs can streamline their financial management, access a wide range of investment options, and optimize their investment returns while enjoying greater convenience and efficiency in managing their finances remotely.

Strategies for Mitigating Currency Risk

Managing currency risk is essential for businesses and investors involved in global transactions. Hedging tools like forward contracts and options can lock in exchange rates for future trades, reducing uncertainty. Diversifying holdings across multiple currencies helps offset losses in one with gains in another. Matching currency cash flows—aligning revenues and expenses in the same currency—also minimizes conversion needs. Staying updated on market trends and geopolitical shifts enables proactive adjustments. Implementing these strategies helps businesses and investors safeguard their financial positions in volatile markets.

Ajit Narasimhan: What are some strategies for NRIs to mitigate currency risk in their investment portfolios?

Krishnan Ramachandran: Reducing currency risk in investment portfolios is essential for NRIs to preserve and enhance the value of their investments amidst currency fluctuations. One strategy is to diversify currency exposure by holding investments denominated in different currencies, thereby reducing reliance on a single currency and spreading risk across multiple currencies. NRIs can invest in currency-hedged investment products such as currency-hedged ETFs or mutual funds, which aim to reduce currency risk by using derivatives or other hedging strategies to offset the impact of currency fluctuations on investment returns.

Analyzing the Growing Potential of Private Credit Markets for NRIs

The private credit market offers a promising opportunity for NRIs looking to diversify their investment portfolios beyond traditional assets. This market has seen significant growth in India, providing non-bank debt financing to small and mid-sized firms that struggle to access traditional funding sources. With returns typically ranging from 12% to 16%, private credit investments can be an attractive option for NRIs. Recent regulatory changes, such as the establishment of GIFT City, have made it easier for NRIs to invest, removing some traditional barriers. The rise of Alternative Investment Funds (AIFs) has also strengthened the private credit space by providing flexible capital to companies with higher default risks. As NRIs move beyond physical assets, private credit presents a compelling opportunity to achieve risk-adjusted returns while participating in India's economic growth.

Madanagopal Ramu: Equities are a well-known market now, but when we talk about alternatives—how do you see the private credit market evolving, where we could see a lot of interest opening up in India? From your perspective, how do you look at it?

Krishna Murthy: From an equity offering, it's relatively easy since data is accessible, and being a fund manager, it's simpler to give 2-3% more than market returns. But in the private market space, I see many people talking about it, and I'm really amazed at how the market has evolved. However, the challenge for NRIs is that when they put money in fixed income at 8-9% interest and then factor in currency depreciation, they end up getting only 5-6% returns. However, in the private credit market, with slightly higher risk, you can achieve better returns compared to bonds or corporate AA paper. The private market focuses on providing returns that are a bit more than BBB paper, targeting 12-16% growth. The risk in credit recovery is mitigated to some extent. With rapid digitization, I see credit risk reducing further. I would personally say that the alternate space has a very good opportunity there.

Navigating Succession Planning and Estate Management

Succession planning ensures a smooth transition of leadership and assets across generations. It involves identifying and grooming future leaders for key roles to maintain business stability. This process often includes training, mentorship, and a clear understanding of the skills required. Estate management, meanwhile, focuses on distributing personal assets through wills and trusts, considering tax implications and legal requirements to minimize disputes. Regularly updating these plans is essential to reflect changes in family, business, or legal contexts. With a solid approach to both, individuals and businesses can secure their legacies and provide clarity for future generations.

Ajit Narasimhan: How can NRIs navigate the complexities of succession planning and estate management across multiple jurisdictions?

Krishnan Ramachandran: Succession planning and estate management for NRIs involve navigating complex legal, tax, and regulatory frameworks across multiple jurisdictions, which requires careful planning and execution. Firstly, it's essential to understand the inheritance laws, tax regulations, and estate planning mechanisms in both the home country and India to ensure compliance and optimize tax efficiency. NRIs should consider creating a comprehensive estate plan that includes wills, trusts, powers of attorney, and other legal documents to outline their wishes regarding asset distribution, guardianship of minors, and healthcare directives upon incapacitation or death. Consulting with legal advisors, tax experts, and estate planning professionals who specialize in cross-border planning can provide valuable guidance and help structure estate plans that address the unique needs and objectives of NRIs and their families. Moreover, maintaining updated records of assets, liabilities, and legal documents in both electronic and physical formats can facilitate efficient estate administration and asset transfer processes across borders. It's also advisable to communicate openly with family members, beneficiaries, and trusted advisors about the estate plan and ensure everyone is aware of their roles and responsibilities in executing the plan effectively. By taking a proactive and comprehensive approach to succession planning and estate management, NRIs can protect their assets, minimize tax liabilities, and ensure a smooth transition of wealth across generations and jurisdictions.

Considering Alternatives and Equities in India

Investing in Indian equities offers strong growth potential, fueled by a growing economy and expanding middle class. Equities can deliver high returns as India strengthens its position on the global stage. Meanwhile, alternatives like private equity, real estate, and venture capital are gaining momentum, providing diversification and lower correlation to traditional markets. These alternatives can act as a hedge during market volatility but often require deeper due diligence due to their complexity. A balanced mix of equities and alternatives can enhance portfolio performance, but aligning with risk tolerance and financial goals is key.

Madanagopal Ramu: As fund managers based in India, we often highlight the country's growth and the strong returns that Indian markets offer to NRIs. However, while the returns might look promising, there are other elements that influence an NRI's decision to invest in India, whether in equities or alternatives. So, from our perspective, what are some of the equally attractive options available to NRIs? And what should they consider when exploring alternative investments in India? It would be great if you could shed some light on that. If you can take us through that, it will be interesting.

Krishnan Ramachandran: From an NRI perspective, the choice today is not limited to India. They're looking at various other options, but various other options also come with a risk-benefit relationship that one has to assess. All said and done, there is always a soft corner for India because they understand India and its growth opportunities. Today, with the information flow happening across channels, almost every minute, even a person in the GCC or the UAE knows what's happening in India in a matter of seconds or minutes. So, there's a good understanding of the Indian market. Many NRIs perceive India as a good investment destination that can deliver returns. There's also a question of looking at alternatives in other global markets, such as debt markets globally, which offer fixed returns. The overriding concern for an NRI always seems to be the rupee-dollar exchange rate. India has been one of the best dollar returns markets in the world, and this is something that we also educate our investors about. We also advise them to consider adding a small portion into alternative markets for a more curated and efficiently managed portfolio. The return perspectives are in the region of between two to five percent, depending on the mix of allocation, and the volatility is also coming down dramatically. So, it's a good scenario for NRIs to look into this alternative space. However, I must say that alternatives have been imprisoned in the GCC markets for the last 13-14 years in one way or the other. That's how the market started in the alternative space through some Indian asset managers or banks running these real estate portfolios. Today, as India becomes more regulated in many segments like the property market or any other alternative segments or the bankruptcy code, NRIs are finding more comfort in looking at the alternative market more seriously.

Key Takeaways

- **Evolving NRI Investment Outlook:** There has been a significant shift from a predominantly India-centric investment approach among NRIs to a more global perspective, reflecting broader opportunities and diversification strategies.

- **Tax Implications and Investment Benefits:** NRIs need to carefully consider the tax obligations and advantages when investing in alternative assets, particularly given the differences between domestic and international regulations.

- **Impact of Global Events:** Events such as the COVID-19 pandemic and geopolitical tensions like the Russia-Ukraine conflict have profoundly influenced NRI investment decisions, highlighting the need for risk management and strategic portfolio adjustments.

- **Utilizing Fintech for Financial Management:** The adoption of digital platforms, mobile apps, and robo-advisors has become essential for NRIs in effectively managing their investments and finances, offering convenience and tailored solutions.

- **Mitigating Currency Risk:** Diversification across different currencies and the use of hedging strategies are critical in protecting investment portfolios from currency fluctuations.

- **Private Credit Market Potential:** Private credit in India offers NRIs an attractive alternative with returns between 12% and 16%. Recent regulatory changes and the growth of AIFs have improved access and flexibility, making it easier to tap into these high-yield opportunities.

- **Succession Planning Across Jurisdictions:** NRIs face unique challenges in succession planning and estate management, requiring careful coordination of legal, tax, and regulatory considerations across multiple countries.

- **Diverse Investment Opportunities:** NRIs have access to a wide range of investment options both in India and globally, including equities, alternatives, and fixed income, each offering distinct risk-reward profiles.

Chapter 03

How Fintech is Reshaping Investment Strategies[3]

- This chapter looks at how fintech influences the wealth management sector. It focuses on using technology to improve access, enhance customer services, handle regulations, and predict future trends.

- Guest Speaker: Mr. Anand Dalmia, Co-Founder & CBO of Fisdom.

  With over a decade of experience in the investment banking realm, Mr. Dalmia has made significant contributions to firms such as Macquarie, UBS, and Avendus. His expertise spans various domains, including M&A, private equity syndication, equity capital markets, and debt financing. Notably, Mr. Dalmia's tenure at Macquarie Capital saw him spearheading their investment banking endeavors and technology initiatives in India. He holds an MBA from IIM Lucknow and a Bachelor's in Commerce from St. Xavier's College, Kolkata.

- Speaker: Mr. Karthik Athreya, Head – Fund Strategy (Private Credit) at Sundaram Alternates.

  Mr. Karthik Athreya is a financial services professional with over 22 years of experience across principal investing, funds management, investment banking, corporate finance,

---

3   This chapter is based on The Alternates Universe episode shot on 24-03-23.

assurance, and transaction diligence services. He heads Sundaram Alternates' (SAA) private credit team which manages assets over USD 275 million in a short span of 5 years, across real estate and private credit.

Foreword

Starting with a passion for wealth creation and sustainable growth, my financial sector journey began as a co-founder of Fisdom, a leading wealth-tech platform in India. Having extensive experience in investment banking from top firms like Macquarie and UBS, my passion lies in utilizing technology and finance to provide widespread access to wealth management services in India. Our mission at Fisdom is to make financial planning easier and provide top-notch wealth management services to all Indians, regardless of where they are located, whether in urban hubs or in the most distant rural areas. Our goal is to provide individuals with the tools and knowledge needed to effectively manage their wealth and achieve their financial goals.

The TAU series has brought attention to distinctive viewpoints, especially on the evolution of financial services in India. What stood out to me was the emphasis on combining traditional banking methods with modern fintech solutions, showcasing the opportunity for collaboration between well-established financial institutions and up-and-coming technology platforms. The show effectively showcased the significance of accessibility and inclusivity, which is consistent with Fisdom's dedication to reaching marginalized markets and offering all-encompassing financial services.

While taking part in the series, I found the conversations on integrating traditional banking with fintech to be especially impactful. They confirmed my belief that the future of wealth management relies on merging the reliability and influence of traditional institutions with the creativity and effectiveness of fintech companies. This mixture is essential for catering to the varied requirements of investors, spanning from high-net-worth-individuals to retail clients, guaranteeing a personalized and tech-savvy method for wealth management. Considering these perspectives has deepened my comprehension of the obstacles and possibilities during this change, as well as the significant potential for expansion and advancement in the field.

The Alternates Universe contributes valuable knowledge to the community by introducing fresh tactics and enhancing comprehension of alternative investments. The show encourages looking ahead, underscoring the significance of adapting to changing market conditions and embracing technological advancements to stay competitive. It also brings attention to the importance of financial literacy and education as the main factors for growth in the wealth management industry. The series has allowed Fisdom to exchange our knowledge with others in the industry, showcasing our commitment to creativity and customer-centric approaches.

In the future, I am hopeful that The Alternates Universe will continue to encourage important discussions and collaboration within the industry. I am looking forward to witnessing a greater emphasis on sustainable investing and the impact of digital transformation on improving customer experiences in the upcoming season. As we move forward, I urge readers to pick up this book and uncover the meaningful observations it offers. It is an important tool for anyone seeking to comprehend the evolving sector of wealth management and alternative investments.

A big shout-out to the creators of The Alternates Universe team for developing a powerful platform that promotes knowledge sharing and encourages innovation.

The Person Behind the Professional

According to several of his colleagues and friends, Mr. Anand Dalmia is described as practical, genuine, empathetic, and, notably, simple at heart, a quality that resonates through his preferences and character. Deeply rooted in Indian culture, he finds solace in the teachings of the Bhagavad Gita and is a fervent follower of cricket, with Virat Kohli serving as a source of inspiration not just for his skills but also his dedication to fitness. Mr. Dalmia's cinematic tastes lean towards action thrillers and grandiose productions, favoring sharp characters over subdued ones. Despite being a staunch vegetarian, he possesses a profound love for North Indian cuisine, along with a weakness for homemade sweets. Recognized for his boundless energy, Mr. Dalmia infuses life into any environment he enters. Adept at conversation, he exhibits exceptional listening skills, embracing diverse perspectives with a non-judgmental approach. While he is known for his firm negotiating stance, he places utmost importance on fostering positive relationships, striking a balance between assertiveness and fairness.

Travel holds a special place in Mr. Dalmia's heart, particularly when shared with his family. He takes pride in his daughter Ananya, who recently earned her black belt in karate, and in his son Ayan, who's acing fourth grade. His wife, Anshu, whom he met at IIM Lucknow, is a yoga trainer and math teacher. Mr. Dalmia's travels have taken him far and wide, yet he finds spiritual fulfillment in exploring destinations within India, such as Mathura, Jagannath, and Vrindavan. Regarded as an exemplary leader by his colleagues, he is admired for his composed demeanor, attentive listening, and empathetic nature.

However, he holds a firm stance against the lackluster effort in the workplace, advocating for a wholehearted commitment to every task undertaken.

Introduction

Financial technology, or fintech, is transforming the wealth management industry to be more accessible, efficient, and personalized. Traditionally, wealth management was exclusive to the wealthy, but fintech like robo-advisors and online platforms have made it available to a wider audience. These innovations use AI and machine learning to offer tailored investment advice, automate portfolio management, and improve user experiences. This shift reduces costs, boosts transparency, and caters to a tech-savvy, younger generation seeking control over their finances. Fintech's evolution is reshaping wealth management, prompting firms to embrace new tech to stay competitive.

Genesis of Fisdom

Fisdom, a leading fintech company in India, was established in 2015 to simplify financial planning and investments for everyone. The platform was created to bridge the gap between traditional finance and the tech-savvy crowd. By using technology, Fisdom provides a user-friendly interface for mutual fund investments, tax planning, and other financial services, helping individuals better manage their finances and reach their goals. Through innovation and a focus on financial literacy, Fisdom has earned a solid reputation in India's fintech sector.

Vikaas M Sachdeva: Anand, what intrigued me when I first met you was your business model. I think your system is very unique. Could you take us to the genesis of this firm and its current scope of product coverage across asset classes?

Anand Dalmia: Certainly, Vikaas. Let me provide some background on Fisdom's genesis. My partner Subramanya and I founded Fisdom in 2015. I came from an investment banking background, while Subbu had experience as a VC investor. We both shared a desire to create something impactful and saw two major themes emerging: the financialization of savings and the disruption of digital in the fintech sector. We realized the challenge of trust, awareness, and inertia in financial services, especially in India, and sought to address these issues through technology. Thus, Fisdom was born, aiming to democratize investing by making it easy and transparent for everyone.

We started with the idea of allowing people to invest in mutual funds digitally, even before the UPI era and the India stack. By collaborating with regulators, we pioneered digital KYC processes, solving transparency and accessibility issues. However, we soon realized the need to address India-specific challenges, leading to the evolution of our unique business model.

Understanding that traditional financial institutions, particularly banks, have unparalleled trust and reach, we decided to collaborate with them. Today, Fisdom partners with 15 banks, including major ones like ICICI, HDFC, and SBI, integrating our tech stack into their mobile banking apps. This approach not only provides customers with the ease of digital investing but also instills trust due to the association with established banks.

Our comprehensive product suite covers various asset classes, ensuring that customers have access to a wide range of financial products seamlessly integrated into their banking experience. This approach has enabled us to reach over 40 crore customers, leveraging the distribution network of our bank partners.

Bridging Traditional Banking and Fintech

The merging of traditional banking and fintech is reshaping finance. It combines established banks' trust and reach with the innovation and efficiency of financial technology. This collaboration boosts banks' digital services, offering customers user-friendly experiences while upholding reliability and security. Fintech firms benefit from banks' customer base and regulatory expertise, scaling their solutions faster. This partnership promotes financial inclusion, enhances customer engagement, and cultivates a dynamic financial ecosystem.

Vikaas M Sachdeva: Your model seems to seamlessly bridge the gap between traditional banking and fintech. However, in the wealth management space, traditional firms have also been successful in building trust and customer loyalty. What gaps do you believe fintech firms like yours are addressing compared to traditional wealth management firms?

Anand Dalmia: Indeed. While traditional wealth management firms have excelled in building trust and loyalty, fintech firms like ours bring a different perspective to the table. One key difference lies in our customer-centric approach. Fintech firms prioritize understanding and solving customer problems at scale, whereas traditional firms may focus more on pushing their own products for revenue generation.

Additionally, fintech firms have a tech-first mindset, leveraging technology to innovate and provide efficient solutions. This contrasts with traditional firms, which may rely more on human intervention and legacy systems. Moreover, fintech firms often prioritize creating value for customers over immediate profit margins, fostering long-term relationships based on trust and service.

Furthermore, our model emphasizes a service layer tailored to different customer segments, ensuring personalized experiences and support. By combining technology with a human touch, we aim to deliver a level of service that surpasses traditional norms, addressing the evolving needs of today's customers.

Understanding Investor Profiles

Understanding investor profiles is key to customizing financial advice and investment strategies to meet individual needs and goals. An investor profile usually includes factors like risk tolerance, investment objectives, time horizon, and financial situation. By evaluating these aspects, financial advisors and wealth management platforms can suggest appropriate asset allocations and investment products that match the investor's specific preferences and circumstances. This tailored approach boosts the chance of reaching financial goals and guarantees a more fulfilling and confident investment journey.

Karthik Athreya: Anand, I find your business model truly fascinating. What I'm most intrigued by is its potential to mediate or intermediate a vast set of customers, especially potential investors. As an investment professional, I'm always interested in understanding the investor profile. Given the massive numbers you're dealing with, I'd love to hear your insights. What is the typical profile of your investor/customers compared to the traditional avenues and formats of wealth management platforms?

Anand Dalmia: Thank you, Karthik. Let me address your question in two parts, starting with the distinction between traditional wealth firms and fintech firms like ours. Traditional firms, driven by their cost structures and revenue focus, typically cater to a certain category of customers, often requiring a significant initial investment, usually starting from ₹50 lakhs or higher. They also tend to concentrate their geographical presence in metro and tier 1 cities, serving older customers with an investable surplus, typically in the age range of 50 to 55 and above.

On the other hand, fintech firms like Fisdom offer a more accessible entry point to investing. With platforms like ours, customers can start investing with as little as 100 rupees in mutual funds or open a free broking account with minimal charges. This accessibility has led to a significant portion of our customer base hailing from tier 2 cities and beyond, constituting around 80% of our users. By leveraging technology, we've been able to break into previously underserved markets, driving substantial growth in mutual fund investments and broking accounts, particularly in the last few years.

This shift is driven by technology, which has addressed the fundamental challenges of trust, inertia, and awareness in the Indian market. Through targeted marketing, educational content, and influencer partnerships, fintech firms have successfully built trust and awareness among mass affluent and retail customers. Moreover, by offering low entry barriers and personalized service, we've attracted a diverse customer base, including those who were previously unbanked or underserved by traditional wealth management firms.

Now, regarding the challenges faced by platforms like ours, regulatory requirements pose a significant hurdle, particularly in a country where multiple KYC processes are necessary for various financial products. This can lead to a high drop-off rate as customers navigate through multiple verification processes. Additionally, there's a historical distrust among customers due to aggressive selling tactics employed by some intermediaries, especially in the insurance sector.

However, our approach at Fisdom is to build trust through transparency and personalized service. By partnering with banks and leveraging their existing customer relationships, we offer a seamless experience that aligns with customers' existing financial habits. This includes providing portfolio reviews and tailored recommendations based on their existing investments, thereby enhancing trust and simplifying the investment process. We pride ourselves on offering a wide range of products without pushing any particular manufacturer or product, ensuring that customers have access to what suits them best.

Technical and Investor Challenges

Navigating the financial sector involves technical and investor challenges that can impact investment success. Technical hurdles like cybersecurity threats, data privacy concerns, and integrating advanced technologies pose significant issues. For investors, challenges include understanding financial products, managing biases, and staying informed during market changes. Overcoming these challenges needs strong tech support, ongoing education, and personalized advisory services for effective and secure goal achievement by financial institutions and investors.

Karthik Athreya: That was a comprehensive answer, Anand. Moving on, I'm curious about the challenges you face both in building your platform and in attracting investors to it. Could you elaborate on the obstacles you encounter from a technical perspective as well as from the perspective of potential investors who may be interested in using your platform?

Anand Dalmia: Absolutely, Karthik. Firstly, from a technical standpoint, building a robust platform that complies with regulatory requirements while providing a seamless user experience is a significant challenge. Ensuring data security, smooth transaction processing, and scalability are paramount considerations in our platform development process. Additionally, integrating various financial products and services into a unified platform requires sophisticated infrastructure and continuous optimization to meet evolving user needs.

On the investor side, one of the primary challenges is overcoming inertia and fostering trust in a digital-first wealth management platform. Many potential investors are accustomed to traditional avenues of wealth management. They may be hesitant to transition to a digital platform due to concerns about security, reliability, and the perceived complexity of digital investing. Addressing these concerns requires proactive education, transparent communication, and a commitment to personalized service to build confidence and encourage adoption.

Furthermore, attracting investors to our platform amidst competition from established players and other fintech firms requires differentiation and clarity of value proposition. We must clearly communicate the unique benefits and advantages of our platform, such as low entry barriers, diversified product offerings, and personalized advisory services, to attract and retain investors effectively.

Overall, navigating the technical complexities of platform development while simultaneously addressing investor apprehensions and competition poses significant challenges. However, by prioritizing user experience, regulatory compliance, and transparent communication, we aim to overcome these obstacles and position our platform as a trusted and accessible destination for wealth management services.

Integration and Accessibility

At Fisdom, we focus on integrating and making services easy to access to bring maximum value to users. By combining wealth advisory services with a user-friendly platform, we tailor personalized recommendations based on your investments, goals, and risk profile. This includes portfolio reviews, investment strategies, and asset allocations. Our platform allows you to easily act on these recommendations for mutual funds, equities, insurance, and more. With intuitive mobile apps and online tools, we empower you to manage your investments efficiently and make informed decisions.

Karthik Athreya: Thank you for the detailed insights, Anand. It's clear that you've identified and are actively addressing these challenges to ensure the success of your platform. Now, I'd like to delve deeper into the integration aspect of your platform. You mentioned earlier that Fisdom serves as both a wealth suggestion/advisory platform and a distribution platform. Could you elaborate on how you seamlessly integrate these functions to provide value to your users? Additionally, what specific strategies do you employ to ensure that investors can easily access and leverage your platform for their investment needs?

Anand Dalmia: Certainly, Karthik. At Fisdom, we've adopted an integrated approach that combines wealth suggestion/advisory services with a robust distribution platform to deliver comprehensive value to our users. Our platform serves as a one-stop destination for investors, offering a wide range of financial products and services, including mutual funds, direct equities, insurance, and more.

To seamlessly integrate these functions, we start by understanding the user's existing investments, financial goals, and risk profile. Through personalized advisory services, we provide recommendations tailored to the user's needs and preferences. This may involve conducting portfolio reviews, suggesting suitable investment strategies, and optimizing asset allocations to align with their long-term objectives.

Moreover, our distribution platform enables users to easily access and execute these recommendations through a user-friendly interface. Whether it's investing in mutual funds, purchasing insurance policies, or trading in equities, our platform streamlines the entire process, from account opening to transaction execution.

To ensure accessibility and usability, we leverage technology to offer intuitive features, such as mobile apps, online portals, and digital tools, that empower users to manage their investments efficiently. Additionally, we provide educational resources, tutorials, and customer support to guide users through the platform and empower them to make informed investment decisions.

Regulatory Compliance and Innovation

Regulatory compliance is crucial for Fisdom's operations, ensuring the platform follows all relevant financial service regulations in India. To gain regulators' trust, Fisdom communicates openly, engages in industry forums, and seeks guidance. The company emphasizes compliance training, helping its team understand regulations and best practices. Technological investments support robust compliance measures like KYC verification, anti-money laundering, data protection, and cybersecurity.

Karthik Athreya: Thank you for that comprehensive explanation, Anand. It's evident that Fisdom is committed to providing a holistic solution that caters to the diverse needs of investors. Now, shifting gears a bit, I'd like to discuss the regulatory landscape. Given the regulatory framework governing financial services in India, what measures has Fisdom taken to ensure compliance and build trust with regulators? Additionally, how do you navigate regulatory complexities while innovating and expanding your platform's offerings?

Anand Dalmia: Regulatory compliance is a top priority for Fisdom, and we've implemented stringent measures to ensure adherence to all relevant regulations and guidelines. Our approach to compliance is multifaceted, encompassing proactive engagement with regulators, robust internal controls, and ongoing monitoring of regulatory developments.

To build trust with regulators, we maintain open and transparent communication channels, actively participate in industry forums and consultations, and seek guidance whenever necessary. We prioritize compliance training and education for our team members to ensure a deep understanding of regulatory requirements and best practices.

Furthermore, we invest in technology and infrastructure to implement robust compliance mechanisms within our platform. This includes KYC (Know Your Customer) verification, anti-money laundering (AML) measures, data protection protocols, and cybersecurity safeguards to protect user information and prevent unauthorized access.

In navigating regulatory complexities while innovating and expanding our platform, we adopt a collaborative approach that involves working closely with regulators to ensure alignment with regulatory objectives and standards. We conduct thorough assessments of new products and features to assess their compliance implications and mitigate any potential risks.

Moreover, we leverage regulatory sandboxes and pilot programs to test innovative solutions in a controlled environment and gather feedback from regulators and stakeholders. This iterative approach allows us to fine-tune our offerings while ensuring compliance with regulatory requirements.

Overall, our commitment to regulatory compliance underscores our dedication to maintaining the highest standards of integrity, transparency, and accountability. By proactively engaging with regulators, implementing robust compliance measures, and fostering a culture of compliance throughout our organization, we strive to build trust and confidence among regulators, investors, and stakeholders alike.

Future Trends in Wealth Management

The future of wealth management is being shaped by several key trends, driven by technological advancements, changing client expectations, and global economic conditions. One of the most significant trends is the adoption of digital technologies, such as artificial intelligence and robo-advisors, which are enhancing the personalization and efficiency of financial services. These technologies allow wealth managers to provide tailored advice and streamline operations, making wealth management more accessible and cost-effective. Additionally, there is a growing emphasis on sustainable and impact investing as clients increasingly seek to align their portfolios with environmental and social values. The rise of alternative investments, including private markets and digital assets, is also transforming the environment, offering new opportunities for diversification and growth. Furthermore, demographic shifts, such as the increasing influence of female investors and younger generations, are prompting firms to adapt their strategies to meet diverse client needs. As these trends continue to unfold, wealth management firms must remain agile and innovative to capture emerging opportunities and address the evolving demands of their clients.

The wealth management industry is changing significantly due to trends like digitization, personalization, and increased collaboration. Fisdom is upgrading its digital platforms for tech-savvy investors, using data analytics and AI for personalized investment strategies. Fisdom is also partnering strategically to build a smooth financial ecosystem and broaden its ESG offerings to meet the rise in demand for sustainable investing. By keeping up with these trends, Fisdom ensures it continues providing value in a rapidly changing situation.

Karthik Athreya: Thank you for that detailed insight, Anand. It's clear that Fisdom's proactive approach to regulatory compliance is essential for building trust and ensuring the integrity of your platform. Now, looking ahead, as the fintech scene continues to evolve rapidly, what future trends and developments do you anticipate in the wealth management industry, particularly in India? How is Fisdom positioning itself to stay ahead of these trends and deliver value to its customers amidst this dynamic environment?

Anand Dalmia: Anticipating future trends and staying ahead of the curve is crucial in the rapidly evolving wealth management industry. At Fisdom, we closely monitor market dynamics, customer preferences, and technological advancements to identify emerging trends and opportunities proactively.

One key trend we anticipate is the continued digitization and democratization of wealth management services. As technology continues to advance and regulatory barriers to entry diminish, we expect to see greater adoption of digital platforms and self-directed investing among retail investors. To capitalize on this trend, Fisdom is enhancing its digital offerings, investing in user-friendly interfaces, and expanding its product suite to cater to the evolving needs of tech-savvy investors.

Another significant trend is the rise of personalized and data-driven wealth management solutions. With the proliferation of data analytics, artificial intelligence, and machine learning, wealth managers can offer tailored investment strategies and personalized advice based on individual risk profiles, financial goals, and preferences. Fisdom is leveraging advanced analytics and predictive modeling to deliver personalized recommendations and enhance the customer experience.

Furthermore, we anticipate increased collaboration and partnerships between fintech firms, traditional financial institutions, and other ecosystem players. By forming strategic alliances and integrating with complementary platforms, Fisdom aims to create a seamless and interconnected ecosystem that offers comprehensive financial solutions to customers.

Additionally, we recognize the growing importance of environmental, social, and governance (ESG) considerations in investment decision-making. As investors increasingly prioritize sustainability and responsible investing, Fisdom is expanding its ESG offerings and integrating ESG factors into its investment processes to meet the evolving needs of socially conscious investors.

Navigating the Regulatory Landscape

Vikaas M Sachdeva: Thank you for that comprehensive overview, Anand. It's evident that Fisdom is taking a proactive approach to adapt to evolving market trends and meet the changing needs of investors. Now, I'd like to delve into the regulatory aspects. Given the regulatory environment in India, which can sometimes be complex and subject to change, how does Fisdom navigate regulatory challenges while ensuring compliance and maintaining operational efficiency? Can you elaborate on the strategies and frameworks that Fisdom employs to address regulatory requirements effectively?

Anand Dalmia: Navigating the regulatory aspects in India requires a comprehensive understanding of the regulatory framework and a proactive approach to compliance. At Fisdom, we prioritize regulatory compliance and have established robust systems and processes to ensure adherence to regulatory requirements while maintaining operational efficiency.

First and foremost, we invest in building a culture of compliance across the organization, with a strong emphasis on ethics, integrity, and transparency. We conduct regular training programs and awareness sessions to educate employees about regulatory developments, compliance obligations, and best practices.

Secondly, we have a dedicated compliance team comprising experienced professionals who closely monitor regulatory changes, assess their impact on our business, and implement necessary measures to ensure compliance. This includes conducting periodic risk assessments, reviewing policies and procedures, and liaising with regulatory authorities to address any inquiries or concerns.

Additionally, we leverage technology to automate compliance processes and enhance regulatory reporting capabilities. By deploying sophisticated risk management systems and surveillance tools, we can detect and mitigate compliance risks more effectively, thereby safeguarding the interests of our stakeholders.

Furthermore, we maintain open channels of communication with regulatory bodies and industry associations to stay abreast of regulatory developments, participate in industry forums, and contribute to the formulation of industry standards and best practices.

Comparing Indian and Global Fintech Firms

The fintech industry in India and worldwide sees rapid innovation and growth, with each region highlighting distinct strengths. Indian fintech companies like Paytm and Zerodha lead in digital payments and wealth management, benefiting from high internet use and supportive regulations. They excel in offering inclusive financial solutions tailored to local needs, such as UPI payments and microloans. On a global scale, fintech giants like Visa and Stripe dominate with advanced payment processing and cross-border transactions. While Indian firms focus on democratizing financial services, global players emphasize scalability and integration across markets. This blend of local innovation and global reach shapes the future of fintech globally.

Vikaas M Sachdeva: Fintechs have changed the way customers access information. How are Indian fintech wealth management firms different from their global counterparts, and are there any unique characteristics of global firms that would be useful for Indian investors?

Anand Dalmia: It's an interesting question. Indian fintechs certainly draw inspiration from global models, particularly those in the U.S., which are often seen as more advanced. However, before comparing differences, it's crucial to understand the varying customer requirements. In the U.S., customers are more financially literate and willing to pay for advice, leading to higher adoption of wealth management services. Moreover, regulations differ significantly between countries, impacting the types of services offered. While India is catching up, there's still work to do in terms of customer awareness and regulatory alignment. However, India has unique advantages, such as lower costs, faster KYC processes, and robust digital infrastructure like UPI. Trends like increasing digital literacy and risk appetite suggest that Indian investors are on a trajectory toward greater adoption of wealth management services.

The Changing HNI Scenario

The outlook for High-Net-Worth-Individuals (HNIs) is changing due to market shifts and regulations until 2023. In India, the fintech sector is booming, with over 9,000 companies adding value to a market worth INR 3.70 trillion in FY 2023. This growth is reshaping wealth management, providing HNIs with personalized, data-driven solutions and better access to digital investment platforms. Globally, fintech advances, like AI and machine learning, are revamping wealth management by offering more tailored and efficient financial services. HNIs are increasingly looking for tech-savvy solutions to manage their wealth, aligning with the trend towards digital and personalized financial management.

Vikaas M Sachdeva: How has the HNI changed over the years, and how has the wealth management space adapted to these changes?

Anand Dalmia: The HNI scenario has undergone a significant transformation. Previously, HNIs relied heavily on advisors and had limited involvement in investment decisions. Today, they are more digitally savvy, demand personalized services, and seek value for money. Wealth management firms have responded by leveraging technology to offer personalized advice, creating tailored portfolios, and enhancing transparency. Additionally, there's a greater emphasis on generating alpha and providing holistic financial planning. The shift towards digital platforms and personalized services reflects the evolving needs and expectations of HNIs.

Aligning Products with Risk-Return Profiles

Aligning products with risk-return profiles is crucial in investment advisory. It helps advisors offer tailored solutions that meet clients' needs. By understanding clients' risk tolerance, goals, and time horizons, advisors recommend products that balance risk and returns. This alignment aids clients in achieving financial goals while reducing losses. Advisors need a solid grasp of investment products, including risks, returns, and correlations with other assets.

Vikaas M Sachdeva: How do you ensure that products offered to customers align with their risk-return profiles, especially when customers may focus solely on returns?

Anand Dalmia: It's a multifaceted approach. Firstly, we employ robust risk profiling methodologies, incorporating behavioral questions to understand customers' risk appetites accurately. Secondly, we leverage data analytics to track customer behavior and preferences, ensuring that product recommendations are aligned with their profiles. Thirdly, we focus on education, emphasizing to customers that returns are relative to their risk profiles and asset allocations. Additionally, we employ algorithms to personalize product offerings, ensuring that customers receive suitable recommendations tailored to their needs and risk appetites.

Emerging Trends in Wealth Management

The wealth management sector is changing due to tech progress and changing customer needs. Firms now prioritize personalization, accessibility, and value creation to offer convenience, personalized financial solutions, and diverse investment opportunities.

Vikaas M Sachdeva: What are the key trends emerging in the wealth management space, and how do you see the industry evolving?

Anand Dalmia: Two significant trends are shaping the wealth management space. Firstly, there's a shift towards integrated experiences, where customers expect access to a wide range of products and services within a single platform. This trend reflects the need for convenience and holistic financial solutions. Secondly, there's a growing demand for "sachet" products, enabling access to investment opportunities for a broader segment of the population. As technology evolves, wealth management firms will continue to innovate, focusing on personalization, accessibility, and value creation for customers.

PSU Banks Adapting to Digital Technology

Public Sector Undertaking (PSU) banks in India are undergoing significant transformations as they adapt to the rapidly evolving digital advancements. Recognizing the need to stay competitive and relevant, PSU banks are investing heavily in digital technologies to enhance customer experiences, streamline operations, and improve overall efficiency. This shift towards digitalization is crucial for PSU banks to remain viable in a market where private sector banks and fintech companies are increasingly leveraging technology to innovate and disrupt traditional banking models. By embracing digital technologies, PSU banks can better serve their customers by reducing costs and ultimately driving growth and profitability.

Vikaas M Sachdeva: How are PSU banks adapting to digital technology in the wealth management journey?

Anand Dalmia: PSU banks are embracing digital technology to enhance their wealth management offerings. They are investing in analytics, digital marketing, and customer-centric platforms like Yono to provide seamless digital experiences. With a focus on open architecture and collaboration with fintech partners, PSU banks are poised to deliver innovative wealth management solutions to a broader customer base. The scale and reach of PSU banks present immense opportunities for collaboration and growth in the wealth management space.

Key Takeaways

- **Technology-Driven Customer Solutions:** Fintech firms, such as Fisdom, place a strong emphasis on solving customer challenges through a tech-first approach, prioritizing long-term value creation over immediate profits.

- **Expanded Investment Access:** Fintech platforms have democratized investing, making it accessible to a broader audience, particularly in tier 2 and tier 3 cities, by offering low entry points and personalized services that cater to individual needs.

- **Commitment to Regulatory Compliance:** Fisdom ensures regulatory compliance through transparent practices, robust internal controls, and proactive engagement with regulators to maintain trust and integrity in the financial services industry.

- **Anticipating Future Trends:** The future of wealth management is expected to see continued digitization, the rise of personalized, data-driven investment strategies, and a growing emphasis on sustainable and responsible investing (ESG).

- **PSU Banks Embracing Digital Transformation:** Public sector banks are increasingly adopting digital technologies to enhance their wealth management services, focusing on analytics, digital marketing, and strategic partnerships with fintech companies to expand their reach and improve customer experiences.

Chapter 04

Emerging Trends in Advisory and Unique Assets[4]

- This chapter details the current trends in advisory and alternative investment spaces, highlighting how technology and diverse investment strategies are reshaping the financial world.

- Guest Speaker: Ms. Lakshmi Iyer, CEO - Investment & Strategy - Kotak Alternate Asset Managers.

With over 22 years of experience within the Kotak Group, Ms. Iyer's expertise encompasses investment advisory and product solutions across fixed income, equities, real estate, and alternates. Previously, she held the position of Head of Products and CIO of Fixed Income at Kotak Mahindra AMC. Before her tenure at Kotak, Ms. Iyer served as a research analyst at Prudence Analytics. She holds an MBA in finance from the Narsee Monjee Institute of Management Studies. She has been recognized as one of the top 25 most influential women in asset management in Asia by an Asian investor.

- Speaker: Mr. Madanagopal Ramu, Head of Equity Fund Management, Sundaram Alternates.

With over 18 years of experience in the Indian Financial Markets, Mr. Madanagopal Ramu currently manages Assets Under Management (AUM) of around Rs. 3500 crores and has over 8 years of experience in managing funds. He manages

---

4   This chapter is based on The Alternates Universe episode shot on 21-04-23.

Sundaram India Secular Opportunities Portfolio (SISOP), Sundaram Emerging Leadership Fund (S.E.L.F.) and Voyager PMS strategies, which have won awards at PMS Bazaar's PMS Rankings FY 21-22 event.

Foreword

With more than 25 years of experience at Kotak Group, I have focused on delivering successful investment solutions in fixed income, equities, real estate, and alternative asset classes, showing my dedication to the financial sector. My transition from working as a research analyst at Credence Analytics to holding the position of Head of Products and Chief Investment Officer for Fixed Income at Kotak Mahindra AMC has been marked by a zeal for creativity and a thorough grasp of investment management. At Kotak, we aim to provide financial solutions that meet our investors' varied needs, establishing enduring connections built on trust and openness.

The series, The Alternates Universe, discusses the continuous advancements in advisory and alternative investments. It depicts the way in which technology and various strategies are changing the financial sector. I am impressed by the series' capability to combine traditional and modern investment methods, which mirrors Kotak's commitment to blending innovation with established financial strategies. In today's complex environment, both advisors and investors need to have a strong focus on adaptability and a thorough understanding of market shifts.

Upon reflecting on my involvement in the series, I discovered the conversations about shifting from mutual funds to alternate assets to be especially enlightening. This change, highlighted by an increased focus on individualized support and the supervision of trust, has been a major aspect of my professional experience. The discussion on asset distribution and incorporating alternative investments into client portfolios struck a chord with me, emphasizing the importance of a well-rounded strategy that caters to a variety of investor preferences. It confirmed my belief that even though technology is crucial in boosting efficiency, the human factor is still vital in offering detailed financial guidance.

The Alternates Universe offers significant benefits to all members of the financial industry by revealing fresh approaches and enhancing the comprehension of non-traditional investments. The show serves as a space for exchanging practical knowledge and examining new strategies for investment management. It encourages financial experts to consider a holistic approach to wealth management, blending both conventional and non-traditional investments to meet the changing requirements of their clients.

In the future, I am excited for The Alternates Universe to further investigate the intricate world of investments and learn more about the possibilities of alternative assets. It would be advantageous to concentrate on how asset manager can better incorporate emerging trends like ESG principles into their strategies, highlighting the increasing importance of sustainable investing. As we progress, I believe this book will encourage readers to evaluate their investment decisions and welcome new ideas with certainty and understanding.

I want to thank the team behind The Alternates Universe for establishing a platform that promotes significant discussions, enriching understanding and awareness in the financial industry.

The Person Behind the Professional

Known for her vibrant personality, Lakshmi's colleagues describe her as bubbly and spontaneous with a sharp sense of humor. A consummate professional, she is admired for her hard work, preparation, and punctuality, regardless of her location. Ms. Lakshmi is an actionist who prioritizes meeting deadlines over perfectionism. She possesses an impressive knowledge of Bollywood movies. Beyond her professional life, she enjoys traveling, exploring nature, and trying new cuisines, with a particular fondness for chocolates and cheese. In her family, she shares her life with her husband and their 18-year-old son, a talented chess player. Together, they dote on their golden retriever, Coco. Despite her busy schedule, Lakshmi remains actively involved in societal affairs. Her achievements in the financial services industry have earned her recognition as one of the top 25 women in India. Fluent in five languages—Hindi, English, Tamil, Malayalam, and Gujarati—Ms. Lakshmi's linguistic versatility is a testament to her diverse background and experiences.

Introduction

Technological advances and changing investment approaches are reshaping advisory and alternative investments. Fintech innovations like AI and data analysis are revolutionizing financial advice, leading to a surge in interest in private equity, real estate, and cryptocurrencies. These assets offer diversification and profit potential. Additionally, the rise of ESG investments highlights a shift towards sustainability. These trends are altering finance, offering new opportunities and challenges for advisors and investors.

Transition from Mutual Funds to Investment Advisory

Transitioning from mutual funds to investment advisory marks a big change in the financial services sector. It highlights the rising importance of personalized financial guidance in today's complex investment world. Fiduciary responsibility, trust management, and transparency are key in both roles. Yet, investment advisory offers a tailored approach to client needs, with a wider array of financial products and strategies beyond traditional mutual funds. This shift mirrors the industry's move towards more holistic wealth management solutions. Advisors now focus on comprehensive financial planning across different asset classes and investment options. The change also stresses the importance of financial professionals adapting to market shifts and meeting evolving client demands. By blending technology with personalized service, they aim to provide value in today's financial world.

Vikaas M Sachdeva: It's been quite a transition for you, moving from a long stint in mutual funds to this new investment advisory role. How has your extensive experience in mutual funds prepared you for this new responsibility?

Lakshmi Iyer: Indeed, Mr. Sachdeva, it feels like I've condensed years of work into just a few months in this new role. My background in mutual funds has instilled in me a deep sense of fiduciary responsibility and the importance of managing trust. Whether it's shareholders or unit holders, they all expect me to be the custodian of their trust. This sense of responsibility is a fundamental aspect of both mutual funds and investment advisory roles. In essence, it's about upholding values, building relationships, and delivering transparent, trustworthy service. I often liken mutual funds to an x-ray, providing transparency into financial health. Similarly, in investment advisory, transparency and trust are paramount.

Asset Allocation and Alternative Investments

Asset allocation is a fine balance that involves understanding clients' return expectations and risk profiles. Alternative investments like Portfolio Management Services (PMS) and Alternative Investment Funds (AIFs) can diversify portfolios, catering to different client preferences. These investments allow for innovation and customization, going beyond traditional routes. It's crucial to set clear boundaries to ensure risks match clients' tolerance levels. By adding alternative investments to a diversified portfolio, investors can boost returns and reach their financial goals.

Vikaas M Sachdeva: That's a profound analogy. Now, as an investment advisor, you're likely dealing with various asset allocation challenges. Where do alternative investments like Portfolio Management Services (PMS) and Alternative Investment Funds (AIFs) fit into your clients' portfolios?

Lakshmi Iyer: Asset allocation is a delicate balance, Mr. Sachdeva. It's crucial to understand clients' return expectations and risk profiles. Some clients prefer traditional, low-risk strategies akin to plain curd rice, while others seek more flavor and texture, like adding fruits and spices. Alternative investments like PMS and AIF offer that extra zest to portfolios, catering to clients' diverse preferences. Additionally, these avenues allow for innovation and customization, offering opportunities beyond traditional investment routes. However, it's essential to maintain a clear Lakshman Rekha, ensuring that risk levels align with clients' tolerance.

Macroeconomic Landscape

The global economy has different trends and changing monetary policies. In the U.S., monetary policy is being cautiously tightened, while India enjoys a positive real rate environment. Investment advisors need to navigate interest rate changes, inflation, and global market trends carefully. Currently, as interest rates stabilize, there might be a shift towards easing, which impacts how investments are balanced between fixed income and stocks. Understanding these economic factors is vital for advisors to create strategies that match market conditions and client needs.

Madanagopal Ramu: Speaking of insights, how do you perceive the current macroeconomic landscape, especially in the context of investment advisory?

Lakshmi Iyer: Mr. Sachdeva, the macroeconomic landscape is akin to "A Tale of Two Cities." Globally, we see contrasting trends, with the U.S. cautiously tightening its monetary policy while India maintains a positive real rate environment. As an investment advisor, it's crucial to navigate these dynamics, anticipating shifts in interest rates, inflation, and global market trends. Currently, we're at a juncture where interest rates seem to plateau, signaling a potential easing phase ahead. This outlook influences investment strategies, emphasizing a balance between fixed income and equity investments.

The Evolving Role of Investment Advisors

Investment advisors are adapting quickly due to tech progress and more investment choices. While tech and AI offer insights and efficiency, personalized advice remains key. Clients now want data-driven strategies and human-centered guidance tailored to their needs. Advisors need to use tech tools while keeping a personal connection to build trust. This means blending technology with personal interactions to navigate finances effectively and provide tailored solutions that align with client goals and preferences.

Madanagopal Ramu: Fascinating perspective. Now, amidst these macroeconomic shifts, how do you see the role of investment advisors evolving, particularly with the proliferation of alternative investment options and advancements in technology?

Lakshmi Iyer: The role of investment advisors is evolving amidst technological advancements and expanding investment options. While technology and AI provide valuable insights and efficiency, personalized investment advice remains invaluable. Clients seek not only data-driven strategies but also human-centric guidance tailored to their unique needs. As advisors, we must blend technological tools with personalized touchpoints, fostering trust and confidence. In essence, it's about leveraging technology as an enabler while maintaining the human touch in client interactions.

Balancing Technology and Personalization

Balancing technology and personalization is important for handling the changing investment advisory. While technology and AI advance, personalized investment advice stays crucial. Clients want data-driven strategies and human-centric guidance tailored to their needs. Investment advisors need to mix tech tools with personal touchpoints to build trust. This approach lets advisors use technology while keeping a human connection with clients, delivering tailored solutions that match client goals and preferences.

Madanagopal Ramu: Your perspective on balancing technology and personalization is insightful. With recent developments such as index inclusion changes and evolving investment avenues, how do you advise clients amidst these shifts?

Lakshmi Iyer: Change is inevitable, and with recent developments like index inclusion changes, it's essential to adapt and innovate. Alternative investment avenues like private credit offer new opportunities for portfolio diversification and yield enhancement. While traditional investment vehicles remain relevant, exploring newer avenues can add value to clients' portfolios. However, it's crucial to maintain a cautious approach, ensuring alignment with clients' risk profiles and investment goals. Ultimately, it's about striking a balance between embracing innovation and preserving stability in investment strategies.

Active vs Passive Fund Management

The debate between active and passive fund management is complex. Passive strategies like ETFs offer investors broad market exposure at low costs but may miss out on the potential gains in dynamic markets like India. Active fund managers use market insights, research, and strategic decisions to outperform benchmarks, crucial in a growing economy like India. Both approaches can be used based on investment goals, risk tolerance, and market conditions.

Vikaas M Sachdeva: Let's delve into the ongoing discourse surrounding active and passive fund management. With the surge in popularity of passive investments like ETFs, how do you justify the continued relevance of active fund management?

Lakshmi Iyer: Certainly, the debate between active and passive fund management is a nuanced one. In my view, both approaches have their respective merits and can coexist within a well-diversified investment portfolio. While passive strategies, such as ETFs, offer investors broad market exposure at relatively low costs, they may not fully capture the potential upside of dynamic markets like India. On the other hand, active fund managers have the ability to leverage market insights, conduct in-depth research, and make strategic investment decisions aimed at outperforming market benchmarks. Particularly in a growing economy like India, where there are ample opportunities for value creation, active management plays a crucial role in identifying and capitalizing on emerging trends and undervalued assets. So, rather than viewing active and passive management as mutually exclusive, I believe they can complement each other, with investors strategically allocating capital to both strategies based on their investment objectives, risk tolerance, and market conditions.

Asset Allocation and Retirement Planning

Asset allocation is a key part of retirement planning. With retirement evolving beyond a fixed endpoint, strategies need to be flexible. Focus on individual goals, risk tolerance, and lifestyle. Instead of rigid age-based rules, aim for specific financial objectives. Use a mix of assets like stocks, bonds, real estate, and alternatives to meet your needs. Take a holistic approach to financial security in retirement.

Vikaas M Sachdeva: Let's pivot to the topic of asset allocation, especially in the context of retirement planning. Given the evolving scope of retirement and longer post-retirement lifespans, how should individuals approach asset allocation to ensure financial security and sustainability?

Lakshmi Iyer: Asset allocation is indeed a critical component of retirement planning, but it's essential to recognize that retirement itself has evolved beyond a fixed endpoint. As individuals retire earlier and live longer, the traditional notion of retirement is being redefined. In this context, asset allocation strategies should be dynamic and adaptable, focusing not just on age but also on individual goals, risk tolerance, and lifestyle preferences. Rather than adhering to rigid age-based formulas, investors should adopt a goal-oriented approach, aligning their asset allocation with their specific financial objectives and life stages. This may involve a combination of asset classes, such as equities, fixed income, real estate, and alternative investments, tailored to meet short-term liquidity needs, long-term growth objectives, and retirement income requirements. By taking a holistic view of retirement planning and embracing flexibility in asset allocation, investors can better navigate the complexities of modern retirement and achieve financial security and peace of mind.

Practical Examples of Asset Allocation

Asset allocation means making a personalized investment plan that fits your financial goals, risk tolerance, and life stages. Instead of sticking to fixed age-based rules, focus on your goals. Mix different assets like stocks, bonds, real estate, and alternatives to meet short-term needs, long-term growth goals, and retirement income.

Vikaas M Sachdeva: So, it's not just about age but also about aligning asset allocation with individual goals and preferences. Could you provide some practical examples of how this goal-oriented approach might be implemented in practice?

Lakshmi Iyer: Certainly. Let's consider a hypothetical scenario where an individual is planning for retirement. Rather than simply allocating assets based on age, this individual takes a comprehensive approach, considering factors such as anticipated retirement age, desired lifestyle in retirement, risk tolerance, and income needs. For example, if the individual plans to retire early and maintain an active lifestyle, they may allocate a higher percentage of their portfolio to growth-oriented assets like equities to capitalize on long-term market appreciation. Simultaneously, they may also allocate a portion of their portfolio to income-generating assets like bonds or dividend-paying stocks to provide stable cash flow during retirement. Additionally, they may incorporate alternative investments like real estate or private equity to diversify their portfolio and enhance returns. By customizing their asset allocation strategy to align with their specific retirement goals and preferences, these individuals can build a resilient and sustainable retirement portfolio that adapts to changing market conditions and delivers long-term financial security.

Reviewing Your Asset Allocation

Reviewing your asset allocation is crucial to keep investment portfolios in line with individual goals, risk tolerance, and market conditions. It's important for investors to review their asset allocation thoroughly at least once a year or after significant life events. During these checks, consider factors like portfolio performance, asset class correlations, economic outlook, and rebalancing needs. Staying informed and proactive helps investors optimize their asset allocation and be flexible in evolving market conditions, ensuring long-term financial security and peace of mind.

Vikaas M Sachdeva: Moving on to the practical aspect of managing investments, how frequently should investors review their asset allocation, and what factors should they consider when making adjustments?

Lakshmi Iyer: The frequency of reviewing asset allocation depends on various factors, including individual preferences, investment goals, and market conditions. While some investors may prefer to monitor their portfolios more frequently, others may opt for a less frequent approach. In general, I recommend conducting a comprehensive review of asset allocation at least annually or whenever significant life events occur, such as changes in financial goals, risk tolerance, or market conditions. During these reviews, investors should consider factors such as portfolio performance, asset class correlations, economic outlook, and rebalancing needs. By staying informed and proactive, investors can ensure that their asset allocation remains aligned with their long-term objectives and risk management strategies.

A Personal Approach to Asset Allocation

A personalized method for asset allocation requires a disciplined review of your investment portfolio, considering your goals, risk tolerance, and market conditions. This strategy highlights the need to avoid impulsive reactions to short-term market changes and to keep a long-term view. By regularly reviewing and focusing on asset allocation basics, investors can confidently navigate market ups and downs to enhance their investment results.

Vikaas M Sachdeva: That's insightful. So, it's about finding the right balance between staying informed and avoiding unnecessary tinkering with the portfolio. Could you share your personal approach to reviewing asset allocation?

Lakshmi Iyer: Personally, I advocate for a disciplined and systematic approach to reviewing asset allocation. I recommend conducting a thorough portfolio review at least once a year, coinciding with tax planning or financial reporting cycles. During this review, I assess portfolio performance, asset class allocations, and any deviations from the target asset mix. If significant market events or changes in personal circumstances occur, I may conduct interim reviews as needed to reassess risk exposure and rebalance the portfolio accordingly. However, I also emphasize the importance of avoiding knee-jerk reactions to short-term market fluctuations and maintaining a long-term perspective. By adhering to a disciplined review process and focusing on the fundamentals of asset allocation, investors can navigate market volatility with confidence and optimize their investment outcomes over time.

Market Volatility

Market volatility poses a constant challenge in finance with unpredictable price changes and investor sentiment. The current equity market resembles a suspenseful movie sequel, keeping investors engaged with unexpected twists. Investors need to make informed decisions amidst market shifts, aiming to optimize their investments in the ever-alluring yet unpredictable world of finance.

Vikaas M Sachdeva: Let's delve into the realm of market volatility. If you had to liken the current state of equity markets to a movie, which movie would it be, and why?

Lakshmi Iyer: I would compare the current volatility in equity markets to the journey depicted in a sequel, perhaps from part one to part two of a movie franchise. Just as sequels often build upon the unpredictability and twists of their predecessors, today's markets are characterized by uncertainty, fluctuation, and unexpected turns. Much like viewers eagerly anticipate the next installment of a movie series, investors grapple with the ups and downs of market sentiment, reacting to each twist and turn with a mix of anticipation and apprehension. Just as movie sequels keep audiences on the edge of their seats, the market's journey from one phase to the next evokes a similar blend of excitement and suspense, reminding us of the enduring allure and unpredictability of financial markets.

Real Estate Investment for Middle-Aged Individuals

Real estate investment can boost a diverse portfolio, especially for individuals in their forties aiming for long-term financial stability. Timing and strategy are key. Consider market conditions, property values, financing, and regulations before investing heavily. For those around 40, align real estate investment with financial goals, risk tolerance, and liquidity needs. A tailored investment plan is crucial for maximizing real estate benefits.

Vikaas M Sachdeva: Real estate has always been a popular asset class among investors. In your opinion, is now the right time for individuals, particularly those around 40 years of age, to consider including real estate as a significant part of their investment portfolio?

Lakshmi Iyer: Real estate can be a valuable addition to an investment portfolio, but timing and strategy are crucial considerations, especially for individuals nearing middle age. While real estate offers potential benefits such as rental income, capital appreciation, and portfolio diversification, investors must assess various factors before committing significant resources. For someone around 40 years of age, the decision to invest in real estate should align with their overall financial goals, risk tolerance, and liquidity needs. Additionally, they should consider market conditions, property valuations, financing options, and regulatory factors. While real estate can provide long-term value and stability, investors should approach it with caution, considering both the opportunities and challenges associated with property ownership. Ultimately, the decision to invest in real estate should be part of a well-rounded investment strategy tailored to individual circumstances and objectives.

Globalization and HNI Investment Trends

The globalization of investment opportunities has led High-Net-Worth-Individuals (HNIs) to explore international investments for diversification and growth. Factors like economic conditions, regulations, currencies, and risks influence this decision. Indian investments stand out for their economic growth, demographics, and evolving regulations, attracting HNIs.

Vikaas M Sachdeva: As we observe increasing globalization, do you foresee a trend of High-Net-Worth-Individuals (HNIs) shifting their investment focus abroad? How might this impact the Indian investment sector?

Lakshmi Iyer: The globalization of investment opportunities has indeed opened up new avenues for High-Net-Worth-Individuals (HNIs) seeking diversification and growth. While some HNIs may explore international investments as part of their wealth management strategy, the extent of this trend and its impact on the Indian investment sector can vary. Factors such as economic conditions, regulatory frameworks, currency dynamics, and geopolitical risks can influence HNIs' decisions to allocate capital abroad. Additionally, technological advancements and access to global markets have made it easier for investors to explore international opportunities. However, the Indian investment opportunities remain attractive, given its robust economic growth, demographic dividend, and evolving regulatory environment. While international diversification can offer benefits such as risk mitigation and access to niche markets, investors should weigh the potential advantages against currency fluctuations, tax implications, and geopolitical uncertainties. Ultimately, the choice between domestic and international investments should align with investors' risk profiles, investment objectives, and long-term financial goals.

Key Takeaways

- **Personalized Investment Strategies:** Investment advisors are increasingly combining technology with personalized guidance to meet the unique needs of their clients, ensuring that financial advice is both data-driven and human-centered.
- **Diversified Portfolio Options:** The rise of alternative investments, such as Portfolio Management Services (PMS) and Alternative Investment Funds (AIF), offers investors more opportunities to diversify their portfolios and tailor strategies to their specific financial goals.
- **Navigating Regulatory Challenges:** Advisors must adeptly manage complex regulatory environments while maintaining transparency and compliance, which is critical in building and sustaining client trust.
- **Adapting to Future Trends:** The advisory space is evolving, with a focus on integrating technological advancements and exploring new investment avenues, such as private credit and ESG, while ensuring that investment strategies remain stable and aligned with client objectives.
- **Globalization and HNI Investment Trends:** High-Net-Worth-Individuals are increasingly exploring international investment opportunities as part of their diversification strategies, which could influence the dynamics of the Indian investment sector.

Chapter 05

Exploring Non-Traditional Asset Classes Globally[5]

- This chapter explores the evolving trends and opportunities in global alternative investments, emphasizing the influence of technological advancements, regulatory changes, and market conditions.

- Guest Speaker: Mr. Umang Papneja, Managing Director and CEO of Julius Baer.

  Mr. Umang Papneja is a seasoned banker with a proven track record and profound expertise in managing businesses of significant scale, size, and reputation. In his current capacity, he spearheads India's growth strategy for Julius Baer, with a primary focus on expanding the firm's local presence. Additionally, he is tasked with driving innovation in product offerings and infrastructure to cater to the evolving needs of High-Net-Worth-Individuals (HNIs) in India.

- Speaker: Mr. Madanagopal Ramu, Head of Equity and Fund Manager at Sundaram Alternate Asset Ltd.

  With over 18 years of experience in the Indian Financial Markets, Mr. Madanagopal Ramu currently manages Assets Under Management (AUM) of around Rs. 3500 crores and has over 8 years of experience in managing funds. He manages Sundaram India Secular Opportunities Portfolio (SISOP),

---

5   This chapter is based on The Alternates Universe episode shot on 26-05-23.

Sundaram Emerging Leadership Fund (S.E.L.F.) and Voyager PMS strategies, which have won awards at PMS Bazaar's PMS Rankings FY 21-22 event.

Foreword

India is witnessing remarkable phase of wealth expansion, with its ultra-high-net-worth individual (UHNWI) segment experiencing significant growth. According to the 2024 Wealth Report by Knight Frank, the number of UHNWI individuals in India is projected to increase by 39% over the next five years, highlighting the country's burgeoning affluent class. As of 2024, India boasts over 210,000 UHNWIs, a testament to the nation's dynamic economic landscape and the increasing accumulation of wealth, driven by strong performances across key sectors such as technology, finance, and entrepreneurship.

Julius Baer stands as India's largest foreign wealth manager, uniquely positioned to serve this dynamic market. Our strategic five-year business transformation, initiated in 2022, is focused on elevating our client franchise, diversifying our product and service offerings, advancing our technological capabilities, and growing our footprint in India. This transformation aligns with the country's wealth trajectory, reinforcing our role as a leader in wealth management and deepening our commitment to India's growth story.

Parallel to India's wealth growth is the rapid evolution of its alternative investment landscape. With projections indicating the industry will expand from USD 50 billion in 2023 to USD 120 billion by 2028, driven by increasing demand for diversification and risk-adjusted returns, alternative investments have become central to sophisticated portfolio strategies. Recognising this trend, Julius Baer is actively developing strategies that align with the evolving market dynamics and investor needs, ensuring our clients have access to innovative solutions that respond to both local and global market shifts.

As India's wealth continues to grow, Julius Baer remains dedicated to supporting our clients in capitalising on these opportunities through our innovative products, robust alternative investment strategies, and valuable insights into the market dynamics that shape their financial futures.

The practicality of the "Alternates Universe" series lies in its focus on actionable strategies rather than theoretical frameworks. This resonates with wealth managers, helping them navigate complex market landscapes while adding value for clients. In future editions, they plan to welcome a deeper examination of regulatory changes affecting emerging markets, as understanding these frameworks is vital for balancing opportunity with risk.

To the readers, I encourage you to engage with the insights presented in "The Alternates Universe" series. This collection offers valuable perspectives for navigating the dynamic financial landscape. I extend my gratitude to the team behind this series for fostering essential dialogues that advance our understanding of the future of wealth management and investment strategies in an ever-evolving world.

The Person Behind the Professional

Mr. Papneja's remarkable ability to connect with people is widely acknowledged by colleagues and acquaintances alike. Described as possessing a rare gift for brevity, he stands out amidst the noise and negativity of today's world. Soft-spoken, down-to-earth, and effortlessly approachable are just a few of the adjectives used to describe him. This aligns with the acquaintance's own experiences, finding Papneja readily available with just a phone call away.

His passion for mathematics and calculations reflects his analytical mindset. Despite being a non-vegetarian, Umang takes pride in embracing his Punjabi roots. Surprisingly, his guilty pleasure is indulging in a steaming hot bowl of rajma. His go-to drink is a neat single malt as a beverage. Cricket holds a special place in Mr. Papneja's heart, with Sachin Tendulkar serving as his ultimate idol. He has two sons whom he considers the pillars of his strength. His love for travel and wildlife is admirable, with the Masai Mara in Kenya being his preferred holiday destination. Above all, Mr. Papneja is a devoted family man, drawing strength from the unwavering love and support of his parents, wife, Yogita, and two sons—they are his pillars of strength. Intriguingly, despite being a true-blue Taurus, Umang possesses a bright, dry sense of humor.

Introduction

Global alternative investment trends are constantly evolving, providing new opportunities for growth and diversification. The advancements in technology, coupled with innovative investment strategies, are transforming the investment world. Alternative assets like private equity, real estate, and cryptocurrencies are becoming increasingly popular, offering diversification benefits and the potential for higher returns. Additionally, the rise of ESG (Environmental, Social, and Governance) investing is emphasizing the importance of sustainability and ethical considerations in investment decisions.

Vikaas M Sachdeva: Mr. Papneja, could you please share some insights about Julius Baer?

Umang Papneja: Certainly, Julius Baer stands as the second-largest Swiss bank, boasting a robust presence in the global financial sector. With assets under management surpassing 430 billion Swiss Francs, Julius Baer holds a pivotal position in wealth management, catering to clients worldwide. The company's listing on the Zurich Stock Exchange underscores its transparency and accountability in financial operations, instilling trust among stakeholders. Notably, Julius Baer's revenue of approximately 4 billion CHF, with a profit margin of around 1 billion CHF, reflects its financial stability and resilience in navigating the market.

The journey of Julius Baer, evolving from its predecessor, DSP Merrill Lynch, to its current stature, exemplifies adaptability and strategic foresight in the ever-evolving financial industry. The transition signifies a legacy of excellence spanning decades, with employees demonstrating unwavering dedication and loyalty. The company's commitment to longevity is evident in its workforce, with many employees boasting over two decades of service. This continuity helps build a rich organizational culture underpinned by experience and expertise, positioning Julius Baer as a trusted partner for wealth management solutions globally.

Vikaas M Sachdeva: Considering your global perspective, what investment avenues do you recommend to your clients?

Umang Papneja: In navigating the global investment environment, Julius Baer prioritizes markets offering sustainable returns, notably the United States and India. These countries stand out for their robust economic fundamentals, conducive business environments, and potential for long-term growth. The U.S. market, characterized by its innovation-driven economy and diverse investment opportunities, remains a cornerstone of many investment portfolios. Similarly, India's vibrant market presents lucrative prospects, particularly given its demographic dividend, expanding middle class, and ongoing reforms.

For Indian clients, Julius Baer emphasizes a balanced approach, leveraging home bias while strategically diversifying into international markets. The launch of a dedicated India Equity Fund underscores the company's commitment to capturing the growth potential of the Indian market for both domestic and global investors. By aligning investment strategies with market fluctuations and client preferences, Julius Baer aims to optimize returns while mitigating risks, ensuring long-term wealth preservation and growth for its clientele.

Growth of Alternative Investments in India

Alternative investments in India have grown remarkably, increasing their share from 9% to 19% in recent years, showing their rising popularity among investors. This growth is fueled by various types of Alternative Investment Funds (AIFs) like private credit strategies, real asset strategies, and private equity and venture capital, which target specific market opportunities and investor needs. The Indian alternative investment market, valued at around $90 billion in 2023, has expanded significantly due to growing wealth among Indian households, rising interest rates, and favorable regulatory changes. Despite risks like illiquidity, volatility, and lack of transparency, these investments offer higher returns and portfolio diversification, making them appealing.

Vikaas M Sachdeva: How do you perceive the growth of alternative investments, particularly in India?

Umang Papneja: The evolution of alternative investments in India reflects a paradigm shift in investor preferences and regulatory dynamics. Since the regulatory changes in 2012, the alternative investment sector has witnessed exponential growth, with assets under management reaching significant milestones. This surge in popularity can be attributed to the flexibility and diversification benefits offered by alternative investment funds (AIFs), catering to both institutional and High-Net-Worth-Individuals (HNIs).

The trajectory of AIF growth underscores a broader trend of investors seeking non-traditional avenues to enhance portfolio performance and manage risks effectively. As traditional asset classes face challenges like market volatility and low yields, alternatives like private credit and long-short funds emerge as compelling options. The increasing sophistication of investors, coupled with regulatory support, bodes well for the continued expansion of the alternative investment market in India, paving the way for innovative strategies and value-creation opportunities.

Interesting Alternative Investment Strategies

Alternative investment strategies provide unique opportunities beyond traditional asset classes, appealing to investors looking for higher returns and diversification. Key strategies include private equity, where investors take significant stakes in private companies to drive growth and profitability; hedge funds, which use various tactics like long-short equity, arbitrage, and global macro to generate returns in any market conditions; and real assets like real estate and infrastructure, offering tangible value and inflation protection. Private credit strategies offer higher yields by lending to non-traditional borrowers, while venture capital focuses on high-growth startups with disruptive potential. Though these strategies come with higher risks and longer investment horizons, they attract sophisticated investors seeking strong portfolio performance and resilience against market volatility.

Vikaas M Sachdeva: Could you elaborate on the alternative investment strategies that Julius Baer finds interesting?

Umang Papneja: Within the alternative investment space, Julius Baer identifies several compelling strategies that align with the evolving markets and investor preferences. Private credit, characterized by its ability to provide consistent returns and diversification benefits, holds significant appeal in the current low-yield environment. Similarly, long-short funds, especially post-taxation changes, offer unique opportunities to capitalize on market inefficiencies and generate alpha.

While private equity remains a dominant asset class globally, Julius Baer acknowledges the attractiveness of listed markets, particularly given the favorable valuations compared to the private market. Real estate and infrastructure investments present tangible opportunities for wealth creation, offering exposure to sectors with inherent growth potential and income generation capabilities. By strategically allocating capital across these alternative strategies, Julius Baer aims to optimize risk-adjusted returns and meet the diverse investment objectives of its clientele.

Diversification Between Traditional and Alternative Investments

Diversifying between traditional and alternative investments helps manage risk and boost returns in a portfolio. Traditional investments like stocks, bonds, and cash offer stability and steady income. Adding alternatives like real estate, private equity, hedge funds, and commodities boosts diversification due to their low correlation with traditional assets. This means that when the market fluctuates, alternative investments can respond differently, reducing overall risk and potentially increasing returns. By mixing these asset classes, investors create a balanced portfolio that spreads risk across different types of investments.

Vikaas M Sachdeva: What is Julius Baer's view on the optimal diversification between traditional and alternative investments? Also, how do you assess real estate investments, particularly in India?

Umang Papneja: While there's no fixed allocation, around 20% of client portfolios are typically allocated to alternative investments. Real estate can be approached through various avenues within AIFs, such as equity stakes in projects, apartment funds, or rental yield strategies. Investing through funds or listed REITs can mitigate operational hassles associated with direct property management.

Gold as an Investment Option

Gold is a popular investment due to its history of holding value and hedging against inflation and uncertainty. It provides security as a tangible asset and is a safe choice during market challenges. Gold diversifies portfolios with low correlation to stocks and bonds. Investors can opt for physical gold, gold ETFs, mutual funds, or gold mining stocks. Yet, drawbacks like storage costs and price volatility exist. Despite risks, gold is a stable component in diversified portfolios, shielding against economic shifts.

Vikaas M Sachdeva: With recent geopolitical events, how do you view gold as an investment option?

Umang Papneja: Gold has gained prominence as a hedge against geopolitical uncertainties, especially with central banks diversifying their reserves. It's no longer just about preserving value against inflation but also about safeguarding against currency risks during geopolitical tensions. If this trend continues, gold could offer returns surpassing traditional inflation-linked expectations.

Private Equity Markets

Private equity markets involve investing in private companies or buying out public companies to remove them from stock exchanges. This strategy aims for long-term capital growth by improving the efficiency, growth, and value of the acquired companies. Private equity firms raise funds from institutions and wealthy individuals, investing in various sectors and business stages, from startups to mature companies. While offering high returns and outperforming public markets, these investments carry risks like illiquidity and the need for active management. Still, private equity presents an appealing choice for investors looking to diversify portfolios and achieve considerable growth.

Madanagopal Ramu: With the recent decline in private equity markets, how long do you anticipate this downturn will continue, and when do you foresee the market picking up momentum again?

Umang Papneja: The current downturn in private equity markets, particularly concerning valuations, is indeed noteworthy. We've witnessed corrections in valuations, especially in tech sectors, where companies were previously trading at unprecedented multiples without significant earnings. However, as time passes and revenues grow, there's been a shift towards more realistic valuations. The expectation of exponential growth has tempered, leading to revised valuations, which have become more rational. This transition from high multiples to more reasonable valuations indicates a normalization of the market.

As for when the market will pick up momentum again, it largely depends on various factors such as economic conditions, investor sentiment, and regulatory changes. However, with the correction in valuations and the significant amount of dry powder available for investment, there's optimism for increased activity in the private equity space in the near future.

ESG Investment Trends

ESG investing in India is on the rise, thanks to regulatory changes, investor awareness, and corporate actions. SEBI now requires companies to disclose ESG info, boosting transparency. Indian investors are embracing sustainable finance and seeking green bonds and ESG funds. The focus on renewable energy, waste management, and ethical business practices shows India's commitment to sustainability. Despite challenges, ESG investments in India are set for growth, supporting global sustainability goals and a stronger economy.

Madanagopal Ramu: That's a comprehensive overview of the current situation. Now, let's shift our focus to ESG investment trends. How do you perceive the importance of ESG considerations in investment decisions, particularly in the context of India's growth trajectory?

Umang Papneja: ESG (Environmental, Social, and Governance) factors have gained prominence globally, and India is no exception. While India is still in the nascent stages of integrating ESG principles into investment decisions, there's a growing recognition of its significance. As a Swiss bank with a commitment to ESG, we acknowledge the importance of sustainable investing practices. In India, while ESG awareness is increasing, there's still a long way to go, especially in terms of regulatory frameworks and market adoption.

However, the trajectory is positive, with initiatives such as the launch of ESG-focused funds and increasing discussions around sustainable investing. Regulatory developments, such as the forthcoming paper on ESG by regulators, further underscore the growing importance of ESG considerations in investment strategies. Ultimately, incorporating ESG factors not only aligns with responsible investing principles but also enhances long-term risk management and value creation.

Role of AI and ML in Investment Strategies

AI and ML are changing investment strategies by improving data analysis, risk management, and decision-making. These technologies process financial data quickly, revealing insights human analysts might overlook. They predict market trends, optimize portfolios, and automate trading for better decisions. AI and ML also analyze news and social media to gauge market sentiment. Robo-advisors make advanced investment strategies accessible to more people. As AI and ML advance, they will enhance performance and reduce finance costs.

Vikaas M Sachdeva: Thank you for highlighting the evolving landscape of ESG investing, Mr. Papneja. Moving on, let's discuss the role of artificial intelligence (AI) and machine learning (ML) in investment strategies. How do you see AI and ML shaping investment products and advisory services in the future?

Umang Papneja: AI and ML have revolutionized various industries, including finance and investment management. While the fascination with using machines to predict market movements isn't new, the advancements in AI and ML present unprecedented opportunities for more sophisticated investment strategies. These technologies enable predictive analytics, risk assessment, and portfolio optimization with greater accuracy and efficiency. However, it's essential to recognize that AI and ML are tools that augment human decision-making rather than replace it entirely. While they excel in quantitative analysis and pattern recognition, qualitative judgment and strategic insights remain valuable contributions of human expertise. As these technologies continue to evolve, they will undoubtedly play a significant role in delivering tailored investment advice and driving innovation in financial services.

India: An Emerging Asset Class

India has emerged as a strong asset class backed by solid economic growth, favorable demographics, and regulatory changes. With a recent GDP growth rate of 8.4%, India proves its resilience as a high-growth market, drawing both local and global investors. SEBI's new asset classes cater to various risk appetites, broadening investment options. Initiatives like the National Single Window System and focus on renewable energy boost India's appeal. Tech, renewable energy, and healthcare sectors show promising growth, making India a key asset class globally.

Vikaas M Sachdeva: Your insights into the integration of AI and ML into investment processes are insightful. Let's conclude with one final question: how do you envision India's position as an asset class for international investors, considering its growth trajectory and valuation compared to other emerging markets?

Umang Papneja: India's growth story presents compelling opportunities for international investors seeking diversification and attractive returns. With a vast and dynamic economy, India offers a favorable environment for business growth and investment. While valuation may fluctuate, it's essential to assess India's long-term potential based on factors such as robust economic fundamentals, demographic trends, and structural reforms.

As India continues to chart its growth trajectory, investors should focus on identifying high-quality businesses with sustainable growth prospects rather than short-term fluctuations in valuations. Additionally, regulatory reforms and initiatives such as the development of GIFT City underscore India's commitment to attracting foreign investment and developing a conducive investment environment. Overall, India's emergence as an asset class reflects its increasing prominence in the global economy and presents exciting opportunities for international investors looking to capitalize on its growth story.

The Role of Technology in the Financial Sector

Technology is changing finance by boosting efficiency, security, and accessibility. Innovations like blockchain, AI, and ML lead this transformation. Blockchain simplifies transactions, cuts costs, and boosts security with a decentralized ledger. AI and ML help analyze data quickly, aiding decision-making and risk management. Fintech solutions like mobile banking and robo-advisors make financial services more accessible. RegTech assists in regulatory compliance efficiently. Tech drives finance toward innovation, efficiency, and security.

Vikaas M Sachdeva: Thank you, Mr. Papneja, for the insightful responses. Now, considering the current economic environment, how do you see the role of technology evolving in the financial sector, particularly in wealth management and investment advisory services?

Umang Papneja: Absolutely, technology is fundamentally reshaping the financial sector, especially in wealth management and investment advisory. We're witnessing a significant shift towards digital platforms, automation, and data-driven decision-making processes. In wealth management, for instance, AI and machine learning algorithms are being utilized to personalize investment strategies based on individual risk profiles and financial goals.

This level of customization enhances client experiences and improves investment outcomes. Furthermore, digital platforms are streamlining operations, reducing costs, and providing greater accessibility to investment opportunities for a wider audience. As technology continues to advance, we can expect even more innovative solutions to emerge, transforming the way we manage wealth and make investment decisions.

Ensuring Data Security and Privacy

Ensuring data security and privacy is crucial in today's digital age. Data breaches and cyber-attacks are on the rise, making it vital for organizations to have robust security measures. This includes data encryption, access controls, and regular security audits. Encrypting sensitive data at rest and in transit prevents unauthorized access. Following the principle of least privilege limits employee access to essential data, reducing internal breach risks. Routine vulnerability assessments and audits help detect and fix security weaknesses. Clear data usage policies and ongoing employee training promote data security awareness. Compliance with regulations like the Digital Personal Data Protection Act of 2023 in India is key to protecting personal data and building consumer trust. By implementing these steps, organizations can safeguard their data and ensure privacy.

Vikaas M Sachdeva: That's indeed fascinating. With technology playing such a pivotal role, how do you ensure data security and privacy in your investment advisory services, particularly with the increasing concerns around cybersecurity threats?

Umang Papneja: Data security and privacy are paramount considerations in our investment advisory services. We employ robust cybersecurity measures to safeguard sensitive client information and ensure compliance with regulatory requirements.

This includes implementing encryption protocols, multi-factor authentication, regular security audits, and employee training programs to raise awareness about potential threats like phishing attacks and malware. Additionally, we adhere to strict data privacy policies to protect client confidentiality and maintain trust. Our continuous investment in cybersecurity infrastructure and proactive risk management practices underscores our commitment to maintaining the highest standards of data security and privacy in all our operations.

Shaping the Future of the Investment Sector

The investment sector's future is influenced by key trends. Investors faced challenges from higher interest rates and inflation, but normalization is expected to benefit equities and bonds. Alternatives like private equity and hedge funds are diversifying portfolios, offering growth opportunities. Technological advances in AI and machine learning are transforming data analysis and trading, enhancing efficiency. Sustainability and ESG criteria are increasingly vital in investment decisions. These trends indicate a more innovative, diversified, and sustainable investment landscape.

Vikaas M Sachdeva: Thank you for sharing those insights into your security protocols. As we wrap up, what would you say are the key factors that will shape the future of the investment sector, both in India and globally?

Umang Papneja: The future of the investment sector will be shaped by several key factors, including technological advancements, regulatory changes, geopolitical developments, and shifting consumer preferences. In India, the continued economic growth trajectory, demographic dividend, and policy reforms will drive investment opportunities across various sectors. Moreover, the increasing integration of ESG principles into investment strategies reflects a growing emphasis on sustainability and responsible investing. Globally, geopolitical tensions, trade dynamics, and macroeconomic trends will influence market sentiment and investment decision-making.

Additionally, advancements in AI, machine learning, and blockchain technology will revolutionize financial services, creating new opportunities for innovation and disruption. Overall, navigating these evolving systems will require agility, adaptability, and a forward-looking approach to investment management.

Key Insights and Recap

- **Focus on Key Markets:** Julius Baer emphasizes sustainable returns by prioritizing investments in significant markets like the U.S. and India, capitalizing on their strong economic foundations and long-term growth potential.
- **Expanding Alternatives:** The alternative investment sector in India has experienced considerable growth since 2012, driven by the need for flexible and diversified investment options that go beyond traditional assets.
- **Attractive Strategies:** Private credit and long-short funds stand out for their ability to offer consistent returns and leverage market inefficiencies, making them appealing choices for sophisticated investors.
- **ESG Integration:** The increasing focus on ESG (Environmental, Social, and Governance) factors is reshaping investment decisions, reflecting a broader shift towards sustainability and responsible investing.
- **Technological Advancements:** The integration of AI and machine learning in investment strategies is enhancing predictive analytics, risk management, and portfolio optimization, leading to more effective and efficient decision-making.
- **India as a Global Asset:** India's ongoing economic growth, favorable demographic trends, and structural reforms are solidifying its position as an attractive asset class for international investors seeking long-term opportunities.
- **Data Security Prioritization:** Ensuring data security and privacy remains a top priority, with comprehensive cybersecurity measures implemented to protect sensitive client information and maintain trust.

Chapter 06

Optimizing Asset Allocation in Alternative Spaces[6]

- This chapter examines asset allocation strategies in the alternative investment space, focusing on optimizing returns and managing risks for Ultra-High-Net-Worth-Individuals (Ultra HNIs). Key topics include ESG investing, technological advancements, and the growth potential of alternative investments in India.

- Guest Speaker: Mr. Saurabh Jain, MD & CEO, Wealth Management, Standard Chartered Bank India.

  Mr. Saurabh Jain leads a comprehensive wealth management business encompassing investments, insurance, foreign exchange, equities, and wealth-leading products. He has been instrumental in driving assets under management, revenue growth, product innovation, governance, and strategic digitalization initiatives.

- Speaker: Mr. Madanagopal Ramu, Head of Equity and Fund Manager, Sundaram Alternate Asset Ltd.

  With over 18 years of experience in the Indian Financial Markets, Mr. Madanagopal Ramu currently manages Assets Under Management (AUM) of around Rs. 3500 crores and has over 8 years of experience in managing funds. He manages Sundaram India Secular Opportunities Portfolio (SISOP), Sundaram Emerging Leadership Fund (S.E.L.F.) and Voyager PMS strategies which have won awards at PMS Bazaar's PMS Rankings FY 21-22 event.

---

6   This chapter is based on The Alternates Universe episode shot on 23-06-23.

Foreword

At Standard Chartered Bank India, our focus is on helping clients manage their finances with precision and confidence. As the Managing Director and CEO of our wealth management division, I lead a team dedicated to designing strategies that strengthen client portfolios and equip them to face unpredictable markets. Over the course of my career, I've emphasized innovation, expansion, and strong governance while also embracing new technologies to enhance client experiences. This approach reflects our ongoing commitment to evolve with the changing needs of our clients in an increasingly complex financial landscape.

The Alternates Universe series plays an important role in making complex investment topics more accessible. I am particularly impressed by how the program brings to light the value of blending traditional and alternative investments to enrich portfolios. This mirrors our own philosophy at Standard Chartered, where we focus on building comprehensive strategies that address the diverse goals of our clients. The series emphasizes the increasing relevance of alternative investments and how these can be integrated effectively to enhance portfolio outcomes. Additionally, the discussions around technology and sustainable investing highlight areas that are becoming increasingly significant for wealth managers and investors alike.

During my participation in the series, I was able to discuss the growing trend of ultra-high-net-worth-individuals incorporating alternative assets into their portfolios. A key takeaway from that conversation was the importance of maintaining a diverse range of investments. Expanding beyond traditional assets like stocks and bonds to include private equity, real estate, and venture capital not only opens up new opportunities for growth but also helps reduce exposure to market volatility. Looking ahead to future episodes of The Alternates Universe, I'm particularly excited to explore the role of artificial intelligence in wealth management and the growing influence of sustainable investing. These are areas ripe for further exploration, and I believe they will play a transformative role in shaping the future of our industry.

Readers will find that this book is filled with valuable insights and perspectives, and they should make maximum use of it. I commend the creators of The Alternates Universe for their dedication to enriching our understanding of alternative investments and wealth management.

The Person Behind the Professional

Mr. Saurabh Jain is known as a hands-on and approachable boss, admired by colleagues and friends alike for his result-oriented and action-driven approach. He is noted for his keen attention to detail and his ability to spot errors, even in the smallest corners of a spreadsheet. Mr. Jain's commitment to staying updated is reflected in his habit of reading up to three newspapers daily despite the information overload of the modern age. On a personal level, Mr. Jain's roots in Kolkata run deep, having completed his schooling at South Point School and his college education at St. Xavier's College. He maintains strong ties with his Kolkata friends, who form a significant part of his social circle. As a passionate sports enthusiast, he enjoys playing tennis, cricket, and football, with his favorite cricket team being the Kolkata Knight Riders (KKR). Notably, he scaled Mount Kilimanjaro in 2016, showcasing his dedication to fitness and endurance.

Being a vegetarian foodie, Mr. Jain loves trying new dishes and experimenting with new flavors. His comfort food is a combination of dal chawal and roti cooked at home. He maintains a health-conscious lifestyle through regular workouts. His family, including his spouse, who heads audit in a large corporate, and his daughter, who recently completed her board exams, are central to his life. Mr. Jain's close relationship with his mother is evident through their annual family holidays. Mr. Jain's guiding principle in life, "*Jitna mehnat, utna meetha phal*," instilled by a Hindi teacher years ago, encapsulates his belief in the correlation between hard work and success.

Introduction

Asset allocation in the alternative investment space has become crucial as High-Net-Worth-Individuals (HNIs) strive to build diversified and resilient portfolios. With a growing interest in private equity, real estate, and venture capital, wealth management professionals navigate the complexities of integrating traditional and alternative investments. They focus on optimizing returns while managing risks effectively, addressing client preferences, and staying ahead of market trends. Balancing liquidity needs with long-term objectives, embracing technological advancements, and incorporating ESG considerations into investment decisions are key aspects of modern wealth management in this dynamic sector.

Ultra HNI Portfolios

Ultra-High-Net-Worth-Individuals (Ultra HNIs) typically have portfolios that are highly diversified and sophisticated, reflecting their substantial financial resources and complex needs. These portfolios often include a mix of traditional assets such as equities, bonds, and real estate, along with significant allocations to alternative investments like private equity, hedge funds, and venture capital. Ultra HNIs also invest in luxury assets such as fine art, rare collectibles, and high-end real estate, which not only provide potential appreciation but also serve as status symbols. Additionally, there is a growing focus on sustainable and impact investing, aligning their wealth with personal values and societal goals. Customized financial planning, tax optimization, and estate planning are crucial components of Ultra HNI portfolios, ensuring wealth preservation and efficient transfer to future generations. The use of advanced financial technologies and professional advisory services helps Ultra HNIs manage their wealth effectively, capitalize on emerging opportunities, and mitigate risks.

Vikaas M Sachdeva: To begin, could you describe what a typical portfolio for an Ultra HNI (High-Net-Worth Individual) looks like in today's landscape of abundant investment choices?

Saurabh Jain: In the case of Ultra HNI portfolios, asset allocation is paramount. Traditionally, a 60-40 split between equities and bonds has been standard. However, recent years have seen a shift towards private and alternative assets, with allocations ranging from 15% to 20%. This diversification serves as a hedge against market downturns and aims for higher returns with reduced volatility. The growth in global alternative asset AUM and India's alternative markets highlights this strategic shift, driven by evolving client needs and risk appetites.

Global Market Outlook

The global market outlook for 2023 is shaped by a mix of economic resilience and challenges. Emerging markets are expected to maintain a growth rate of 4.2%, consistent with 2022, while developed markets face potential tightening policies to control inflation, which could lead to synchronized recessions by the end of 2024. Despite these risks, sectors like technology and renewable energy present growth opportunities, especially in regions like Asia, which are projected to experience stronger growth and lower inflation compared to the U.S. and Europe. The U.S. market, buoyed by solid corporate earnings and moderated inflation, saw a 25% rally in stocks, particularly in technology and growth sectors, driven by expectations of rate cuts in 2024. Investors are advised to remain selective, focusing on defensive stocks in the U.S. and Europe while exploring high-growth opportunities in Japan and emerging markets. Overall, while economic uncertainties persist, strategic investments in resilient and growth-oriented sectors can offer attractive returns.

Vikaas M Sachdeva: You also mentioned a recent report on the global market outlook. Could you provide more insights into the key findings of this report and its implications for investors?

Saurabh Jain: Our report, "Calm," advocates for a balanced approach amidst divergent market sentiments. Diversification is crucial, focusing on global equities, particularly in Asia ex-Japan, and investment-grade bonds in developed markets. We see promise in China's market despite challenges and remain bullish on India's growth driven by demographic trends and policy reforms. Prudence, adaptability, and a global perspective are essential to navigate today's investment landscape effectively.

India's Equity Market

India's equity market has demonstrated remarkable resilience and growth, positioning itself as one of the best-performing markets globally. The Nifty 50 and S&P BSE Sensex indices have seen substantial gains of approximately 18% and 21%, respectively, driven by strong corporate earnings, particularly in the technology and automotive sectors. Foreign Portfolio Investors (FPIs) have shown renewed confidence, with net inflows reaching $12.6 billion, significantly higher than other emerging markets. The market capitalization of companies listed on Indian exchanges surpassed $4 trillion for the first time, making India the fifth-largest equity market in the world. Key sectors such as real estate, capital goods, and automobiles have led the rally, supported by government initiatives and robust domestic demand. Despite global economic challenges, including inflation and geopolitical tensions, India's focus on infrastructure development and manufacturing has bolstered investor sentiment, setting a positive outlook for continued growth in the equity market.

Vikaas M Sachdeva: Could you delve deeper into your assessment of India's equity market and the rationale behind maintaining a neutral stance in your portfolio allocation?

Saurabh Jain: While India shows strong earnings growth and favorable macroeconomic indicators, high valuations and potential headwinds like high interest rates warrant caution. Our neutral stance balances optimism about India's long-term growth with concerns about valuation levels. By maintaining a neutral stance, we capitalize on growth opportunities while mitigating risks associated with market volatility and valuation uncertainties.

ESG Investing Trends

ESG (Environmental, Social, and Governance) investing trends have continued to evolve, driven by regulatory changes, increased investor scrutiny, and a growing emphasis on sustainability. Key trends include a heightened focus on ethics and integrity, with organizations under pressure to ensure their ESG claims are credible and not mere greenwashing. Investors are demanding more transparent and data-backed ESG disclosures to assess performance accurately. Additionally, there is a significant push towards addressing climate change risks, with companies setting more ambitious net-zero targets and enhancing their transition plans. The use of advanced technologies, such as data analytics and AI, is becoming central to ESG strategies, enabling better risk management and performance tracking. Despite some backlash and regulatory challenges, particularly in the U.S., the overall momentum towards integrating ESG principles into investment decisions remains strong, reflecting a broader commitment to sustainable and responsible investing.

Vikaas M Sachdeva: Could you elaborate on the evolving trends and investor preferences in the ESG (Environmental, Social, and Governance) investing space?

Saurabh Jain: ESG investing is gaining traction, reflecting a growing awareness of sustainability and responsible investing. Our wealth expectancy report shows over 50% of clients prefer ESG-oriented investments. While the adoption of ESG principles varies, there's a clear trend towards integrating sustainability considerations into investment strategies. This shift aligns financial objectives with broader societal and environmental goals, enhancing long-term investment outcomes.

Generative AI and Wealth Management

Generative AI is significantly transforming wealth management by enhancing efficiency, personalization, and decision-making processes.

By leveraging advanced algorithms, generative AI can analyze vast amounts of financial data, generate insights, and create tailored investment strategies for clients. It improves customer engagement through AI-powered virtual assistants that provide personalized financial advice and real-time portfolio adjustments. Additionally, generative AI automates routine tasks such as document management, compliance monitoring, and report generation, freeing up wealth managers to focus on strategic activities. The technology also aids in identifying and prioritizing potential clients by analyzing both structured and unstructured data, making marketing efforts more effective. As the adoption of generative AI grows, it promises to elevate the capabilities of wealth management firms, driving better client outcomes and operational efficiencies.

Madanagopal Ramu: Regarding the view on generative AI and its potential impact on financial services, especially in wealth management. What are your insights on this?

Saurabh Jain: AI and technological advancements are reshaping wealth management, democratizing financial advice and enhancing client engagement. While chatbots and AI tools can handle routine tasks, they cannot replace the nuanced trust dynamics between clients and advisors. We leverage technology to enhance advisory capabilities, offering personalized insights and optimizing portfolio performance through data-driven recommendations.

Alternative Investments and Illiquidity

Alternative investments, including assets like private equity, real estate, hedge funds, and commodities, offer diversification benefits but come with the challenge of illiquidity. Unlike traditional investments such as stocks and bonds, alternative assets often cannot be easily sold or converted to cash without a significant loss in value. This illiquidity arises because these investments typically have fewer buyers and sellers, leading to larger bid-ask spreads and greater price volatility. While illiquid assets can potentially offer higher returns due to a liquidity premium, investors must be prepared for longer holding periods and the inability to quickly access their capital. Therefore, thorough due diligence and a clear understanding of one's liquidity needs are crucial when incorporating alternative investments into a portfolio.

Vikaas M Sachdeva: There's often concern regarding illiquidity in alternative investments. How does Standard Chartered address this concern while advising clients?

Saurabh Jain: Illiquidity in alternative investments is a challenge, but it can be mitigated through portfolio diversification and risk management. By allocating a portion of the portfolio to alternative assets like private equity and venture capital, clients can enhance returns and mitigate volatility. Our approach emphasizes prudent allocation across liquid and illiquid assets, balancing liquidity needs with long-term investment objectives.

New-Age HNIs and Investment Preferences

New-age High-Net-Worth-Individuals (HNIs) are redefining investment preferences by prioritizing innovation, sustainability, and diversification. Unlike traditional HNIs, they are more inclined towards technology-driven sectors such as fintech, biotech, and renewable energy, reflecting their comfort with digital transformation and future-oriented industries. They also show a strong preference for impact investing, seeking opportunities that align with their values and contribute positively to society and the environment. Additionally, new-age HNIs are leveraging advanced financial technologies, including robo-advisors and AI-driven analytics, to make informed investment decisions. They value personalized financial advice and are willing to explore alternative investments like venture capital, private equity, and cryptocurrencies to achieve higher returns and diversify their portfolios. This shift highlights a more proactive, informed, and socially conscious approach to wealth management among the new generation of HNIs.

Vikaas M Sachdeva: How do new-age HNIs' investment preferences differ, especially concerning alternative investments and risk appetite?

Saurabh Jain: New-age HNIs exhibit a higher risk appetite and greater exposure to alternative investments like cryptocurrencies and venture capital. They are more informed and receptive to innovative investment avenues, and they also prioritize wealth preservation. We tailor bespoke solutions to align with their preferences while ensuring a holistic approach to portfolio management.

Technology and Portfolio Management

Technology is revolutionizing portfolio management by enhancing efficiency, precision, and personalization. Advanced tools such as artificial intelligence (AI) and machine learning (ML) enable the analysis of vast datasets, providing deeper insights and more accurate predictions for investment strategies. Automated trading systems streamline the execution of trades, reduce human error, and optimize transaction costs. Real-time data analytics offer portfolio managers the ability to make informed decisions swiftly, adjusting strategies to align with market conditions. Additionally, technology facilitates personalized investment advice through robo-advisors and AI-driven platforms, making sophisticated financial planning accessible to a broader audience. These advancements not only improve operational efficiency but also enhance client satisfaction by offering tailored solutions and transparent, data-backed investment decisions.

Vikaas M Sachdeva: There's interest in the role of technology in portfolio management. What's your take on the feasibility of dedicated fund managers catering to individual investor inputs for mass customization?

Saurabh Jain: Mass customization in portfolio management is promising, leveraging technology to tailor investment solutions to individual investor preferences. At Standard Chartered, we combine technological innovation with expert guidance to offer customized solutions, ensuring alignment with client goals and risk profiles.

Global Financial Trends and Gold

In 2023, global financial trends have highlighted the importance of gold as a strategic investment. Despite a slowdown in global GDP growth to 2.9% due to high interest rates and inflationary pressures, gold has shown resilience, ending the year at a record-high price of $2,078.4 per ounce, with an annual return of 15%. Central banks continued their robust gold purchasing, nearly matching the record levels of 2022, while gold's role as a hedge against inflation and economic uncertainty remained prominent. Investment in gold bars and coins saw varied trends across regions, with strong demand in China and Turkey offsetting declines in Europe due to rising interest rates. As a highly liquid and globally accepted asset, gold provides portfolio diversification and stability, making it an attractive option for investors looking to mitigate risks in a volatile economic environment.

Vikaas M Sachdeva: How does Standard Chartered view the dynamics of currency wars and the attractiveness of gold amidst potential de-dollarization efforts?

Saurabh Jain: Currency wars and de-dollarization efforts underscore shifting global financial dynamics. Gold remains a traditional safe haven asset, offering portfolio diversification. Our outlook considers currency trends, geopolitical developments, and economic indicators to formulate prudent investment strategies that safeguard client interests while optimizing risk-adjusted returns.

Future Trajectory of Alternative Investments in India

The future trajectory of alternative investments in India is poised for substantial growth, driven by increasing investor interest and regulatory support. The share of alternatives in the asset management industry has surged from 9% to 19%, reflecting their growing appeal. Key segments include Alternative Investment Funds (AIFs), Infrastructure Investment Trusts (InvITs), and Real Estate Investment Trusts (REITs). These vehicles offer diversified investment opportunities across private credit, real assets, and private equity/venture capital. Private credit strategies provide debt capital to businesses where traditional lenders are constrained, while real asset strategies focus on infrastructure and real estate. Private equity and venture capital continue to fuel business growth by providing critical funding at various stages. The expertise and active management by specialized teams enhance the value of these investments. As India continues to develop its financial markets, alternative investments are expected to play a crucial role in driving economic growth and offering robust returns to investors willing to navigate their inherent illiquidity and longer investment horizons.

Vikaas M Sachdeva: How does Standard Chartered envision the future trajectory of the alternative investments sector in India compared to global markets?

Saurabh Jain: India's alternative investments sector is growing rapidly, driven by regulatory reforms and increased investor participation. While it may take time to reach global market levels, the trajectory is promising, fueled by rising investor appetite for innovative investment avenues. Our focus is harnessing this potential to offer diverse investment opportunities that cater to evolving client needs while adhering to regulatory standards.

Key Takeaways

- **Enhanced Diversification Strategies:** Ultra HNI portfolios are shifting towards a more diversified approach, incorporating private equity, hedge funds, and other alternative assets to manage risks and target higher returns. This evolution reflects a move away from traditional asset allocations, aiming to mitigate market volatility.

- **Global Market Strategy:** A balanced investment approach focusing on global equities, particularly in emerging markets like Asia ex-Japan, and investment-grade bonds in stable economies is recommended. This strategy leverages growth opportunities in dynamic sectors while maintaining defensive positions in established markets. India's market remains promising but requires a measured approach due to high valuations.

- **Growing Importance of ESG:** ESG (Environmental, Social, and Governance) investing is gaining traction, with increasing client demand for investments that align with sustainability and ethical principles. This trend is shaping how wealth is managed as investors seek to balance financial returns with positive societal impact.

- **Role of AI in Wealth Management:** The integration of AI and machine learning is enhancing wealth management by offering more personalized financial advice and improving portfolio performance. These technologies are making advanced investment strategies more accessible, optimizing decision-making processes.

- **Managing Illiquidity in Alternatives:** While alternative investments offer diversification and the potential for higher returns, they come with challenges like illiquidity. Prudent allocation across liquid and illiquid assets is crucial to ensure that clients' liquidity needs are met alongside long-term investment goals.

- **New-Age HNI Preferences:** Modern HNIs show a greater appetite for risk and are more inclined towards innovative investments, such as cryptocurrencies and venture capital. Their investment strategies require customized solutions that cater to their unique preferences and broader exposure to alternative assets.

- **Gold as a Strategic Investment:** Amidst global financial shifts and discussions around de-dollarization, gold continues to serve as a valuable hedge, offering stability and diversification in investment portfolios.

- **Growth of Alternatives in India:** The alternative investment sector in India is expanding, driven by regulatory support and increasing investor interest. This growth presents new opportunities for those looking to diversify their portfolios and achieve long-term value.

Chapter 07

Proven Methods for Financial Growth and Sustainability[7]

- This chapter explores successful wealth management strategies, highlighting technology's role in enhancing relationships with clients, the strategic use of leverage by HNIs and Ultra HNIs, and the impact of regulatory and technological changes.

- Guest Speaker: Mr. Anupam Guha*, Head of Private Equity Management, ICICI Securities Limited.

  With an illustrious career spanning over 19 years within the ICICI Group, Mr. Guha has cultivated expertise across retail, institutional, and private banking sectors, including a significant tenure overseeing private wealth management both in India and abroad. He stands as one of the pioneering architects behind the establishment of the private wealth management division at ICICI Securities.

- Speaker: Mr. Karthik Athreya, Head – Fund Strategy (Private Credit) at Sundaram Alternates.

  Mr. Karthik Athreya is a financial services professional with over 22 years of experience across principal investing, funds management, investment banking, corporate finance, assurance, and transaction diligence services. He heads Sundaram Alternates' (SAA) private credit team which manages assets over USD 275 million in a short span of 5 years, across real estate and private credit.

---

7   This chapter is based on The Alternates Universe episode shot on 28-07-23.

*   The speaker has transitioned to a leadership role at a private wealth firm.

The Person Behind the Professional

Mr. Guha is deeply passionate about running, transcending mere passion to become an integral aspect of his identity. An avid marathoner, his journey commenced with a remarkable feat: conquering his first half marathon in 2017, followed swiftly by a full marathon in 2018. Yet, Mr. Guha's pursuit of excellence knew no bounds, culminating in the triumph of completing the grueling Comrades Marathon in South Africa not once but twice in 2019. Beyond athletics, Mr. Guha's intellectual pursuits shine brightly. An ardent reader and dedicated workaholic, his commitment to a disciplined lifestyle governed by a rigorous dietary regimen echoes the ethos of his running endeavors. A connoisseur of fish, not merely for sustenance but for its high protein content, Mr. Guha epitomizes the embodiment of Sagittarian tenacity with a zest for life that resonates deeply among his peers.

Within the corridors of ICICI Bank, where Mr. Guha began his professional odyssey, his leadership prowess reigns supreme. With an uncanny ability to navigate the intricacies of business from a panoramic perspective down to the minutiae of operational trenches, his colleagues attest to his unparalleled acumen. A seasoned ICICI lifer, Mr. Guha's tenure spans decades, a testament not only to the institution but also to his exceptional leadership qualities that inspire loyalty and admiration. Furthermore, Mr. Guha's networking prowess and adeptness in relationship management are legendary within the ICICI fold. Balancing client engagements with internal collaborations seamlessly, he orchestrates a symphony of success that resonates throughout the organization.

Away from the boardrooms and marathons, Mr. Guha finds solace in familial bonds and community engagement. A devoted family man with a penchant for travel and instrumental music, his household resonates with creativity, evident in his wife's and children's talents. Rooted in an army background, Mr. Guha's zest for life and outgoing demeanor reflect the indomitable spirit inherited from his father and brother. His nomadic upbringing instilled a wanderlust that continues to fuel his adventures.

Amidst the intensity of his professional endeavors, Mr. Guha's friends attest to his delightfully eccentric sense of humor, offering a glimpse into the lighthearted dimension of his persona. Yet, beneath the surface lies a man deeply passionate by diligence and commitment, a sentiment mirrored in his professional achievements, notably steering ICICI Securities to remarkable heights of success.

Introduction

Successful wealth management strategies for High-Net-Worth-Individuals (HNIs) and Ultra HNIs hinge on leveraging technology, understanding the balance of risks and rewards, and adapting to regulatory and technological changes. Technology plays a pivotal role in enhancing relationship management by providing advanced tools and insights that allow for more personalized and precise advice. This personalization strengthens client relationships and builds trust. Additionally, the strategic use of leverage can significantly amplify returns, though it requires careful risk management to mitigate potential downsides. Aligning wealth management models with clients' interests is crucial, as it ensures that financial advisors act in the best interests of their clients, fostering transparency and trust. Adapting to regulatory shifts and embracing technological advancements further solidifies a wealth management firm's ability to provide exceptional service and maintain a competitive edge. This comprehensive approach to wealth management underscores the importance of technology, strategic planning, and client-centric models in achieving long-term financial success for HNIs and Ultra HNIs.

Insights on Wealth Management and Technology

The integration of technology in wealth management is transforming the role of relationship managers by enhancing their capabilities and shifting their focus towards more strategic and personalized client interactions. Advanced technologies such as artificial intelligence (AI) and machine learning (ML) are automating routine tasks like portfolio rebalancing, transaction processing, and data analysis, allowing relationship managers to dedicate more time to understanding and addressing the unique needs of their clients. Digital platforms and predictive analytics provide real-time insights and tailored investment recommendations, enabling relationship managers to offer more informed and customized advice. Additionally, technology facilitates seamless communication through virtual meetings and client portals, improving accessibility and engagement. While these advancements streamline operations and improve efficiency, they also require relationship managers to adapt by developing new skills and embracing a more tech-savvy approach to client management. This evolution ultimately enhances the client experience, making wealth management more responsive and personalized.

Vikaas M Sachdeva: How has technology helped your relationship managers (RMs) in the wealth management industry?

Anupam Guha: Technology has been transformative for our RMs in the wealth management industry. It's not just about replacing traditional methods but enhancing human capabilities with advanced tools and insights. With technology, RMs can uncover patterns and preferences in client data that were previously inaccessible. This allows them to tailor their advice and recommendations with unprecedented precision, creating stronger and more personalized client relationships.

Furthermore, technology provides RMs with real-time access to market trends, investment opportunities, and portfolio performance, empowering them to make informed decisions. By leveraging cutting-edge platforms and analytics, RMs can offer proactive guidance, anticipate client needs, and deliver value-added solutions that drive long-term financial success.

Vikaas M Sachdeva: Given the traditional nature of relationship-based businesses, how do your RMs perceive the integration of technology into their roles?

Anupam Guha: The integration of technology into our RMs' roles has seen mixed reactions, from enthusiasm to apprehension. Initially, some RMs viewed technology as a threat to their traditional methods. However, as they witnessed the tangible benefits, their perception shifted. They began to see technology not as a replacement but as a powerful tool that amplifies their capabilities and efficiency.

Our organization has proactively upskilled our RMs, providing comprehensive training and support to ensure they can leverage technology effectively. By encouraging a culture of continuous learning and adaptation, we've cultivated a workforce that embraces innovation and maximizes the potential of technology to deliver exceptional value to our clients.

Vikaas M Sachdeva: How do you ensure that your RMs effectively utilize the technology tools available to them?

Anupam Guha: Ensuring effective utilization of technology tools among our RMs requires a strategic approach. We provide comprehensive training and ongoing support to familiarize RMs with the features and functionalities of the technology tools. This includes hands-on workshops, online tutorials, and access to dedicated support channels.

We emphasize integrating technology into their daily workflows by showcasing real-world examples of how these tools can streamline processes, enhance productivity, and drive better outcomes for both clients and the business. Additionally, we encourage a culture of continuous learning and innovation, prompting RMs to explore new technologies, share best practices, and collaborate with peers.

Understanding Leverage in Wealth Generation

Leverage in wealth generation refers to the use of borrowed capital to increase the potential return on investment. High-Net-Worth-Individuals (HNIs) and Ultra-High-Net-Worth-Individuals (Ultra HNIs) typically utilize leverage to amplify their investment opportunities and enhance wealth creation. By borrowing funds at a lower interest rate than the expected return on their investments, they can invest in a broader range of assets, such as real estate, private equity, and hedge funds. This strategy allows them to control larger positions with a relatively small amount of their own capital, potentially leading to higher returns. However, leverage also comes with increased risk, as it can magnify losses if investments do not perform as expected. To manage this risk,

HNIs and Ultra HNIs often employ sophisticated financial strategies and work with professional advisors to carefully assess the risk-reward balance and ensure that their leverage is used effectively to achieve their financial goals.

Vikaas M Sachdeva: What is leverage, and how do HNIs and Ultra HNIs typically utilize it to enhance their wealth generation?

Anupam Guha: Leverage in finance is akin to walking a tightrope; it magnifies both gains and losses. Accredited investors, including High-Net-Worth-Individuals (HNIs) and Ultra-High-Net-Worth-Individuals (Ultra HNIs), often leverage their capital strategically to amplify returns. However, it's crucial to exercise caution, as leverage can exacerbate market volatility and lead to substantial losses if not managed prudently. These sophisticated investors, often supported by professional advisors, employ leverage judiciously, aligning it with their investment objectives and risk appetite. By striking a delicate balance between risk and reward, they aim to optimize portfolio performance while safeguarding against potential downsides.

Vikaas M Sachdeva: What are the risks associated with leveraging investments, and how can accredited investors navigate these challenges effectively?

Anupam Guha: Leveraging investments introduces a layer of complexity that demands meticulous risk management, particularly for accredited investors. While leverage has the potential to enhance returns, it also amplifies the magnitude of losses in adverse market conditions. Accredited investors must be aware of these risks and adopt robust risk mitigation strategies to protect their capital. This entails diversifying their investment portfolios, setting strict risk limits, and regularly monitoring market dynamics. By employing a disciplined approach to leverage, accredited investors can mitigate downside risks while capitalizing on opportunities for wealth creation in volatile markets.

Balancing Risks and Benefits

Accredited investors balance the potential benefits of leveraging with inherent risks by employing a combination of sophisticated strategies and diligent risk management. Leverage allows them to amplify returns by using borrowed capital to increase their investment capacity. However, it also magnifies potential losses, making risk assessment crucial. Accredited investors typically diversify their portfolios across various asset classes, including private equity, hedge funds, and real estate, to spread risk. They also conduct thorough due diligence, analyzing the financial health and growth prospects of potential investments. Additionally, they often work with experienced financial advisors to create tailored strategies that align with their risk tolerance and financial goals. By carefully monitoring their leveraged positions and maintaining adequate liquidity, accredited investors can mitigate risks while maximizing the benefits of leveraging to enhance their wealth generation.

Karthik Athreya: In the context of wealth management, how do accredited investors balance the potential benefits of leveraging with the inherent risks involved?

Anupam Guha: Wealth management for accredited investors hinges on striking a delicate balance between leveraging opportunities and risk mitigation strategies. While leveraging can amplify returns, it also exposes investors to heightened market volatility and liquidity risks. Accredited investors, often guided by seasoned financial advisors, assess the risk-return profile of leveraging strategies and tailor them to align with their investment goals and risk tolerance. By diversifying across asset classes, employing leverage judiciously, and maintaining a long-term perspective, these investors aim to optimize portfolio performance while safeguarding against undue risks. Ultimately, successful wealth management for accredited investors entails meticulous planning, disciplined execution, and a thorough understanding of the complexities associated with leveraging investments.

Navigating Technological Hazards

Navigating technological hazards requires a comprehensive approach to risk management and preparedness. Technological hazards encompass a wide range of incidents, including hazardous materials spills, nuclear power plant failures, industrial pollution, and cyber-attacks. These hazards often occur with little or no warning and can have long-term health and environmental impacts. Effective strategies to mitigate these risks include thorough planning, regular training, and community awareness programs. Local Emergency Planning Committees (LEPCs) play a crucial role in collecting information about hazardous materials, developing emergency response plans, and educating the public on safety measures. Organizations must also implement robust technology risk management practices, which involve identifying potential risks, conducting regular audits, and maintaining up-to-date security protocols. By proactively addressing these hazards, communities and businesses can better protect themselves from the adverse effects of technological incidents.

Karthik Athreya: How do wealth managers like you navigate technological hazards such as phishing, SIM switch fraud, and other cyber threats to protect clients' assets effectively?

Anupam Guha: Mitigating technological hazards in wealth management requires a multifaceted approach centered on robust cybersecurity measures and proactive risk management. Wealth managers leverage advanced encryption protocols, multi-factor authentication systems, and secure communication channels to safeguard clients' sensitive financial information from phishing attacks and unauthorized access. Additionally, ongoing cybersecurity awareness training equips wealth management teams with the knowledge and skills needed to identify and thwart emerging cyber threats effectively. Moreover, close collaboration with regulatory authorities and industry partners enables wealth managers to stay updated on cybersecurity best practices and regulatory guidelines, ensuring robust protection of clients' assets in an increasingly digitized financial environment.

Advisory vs. Commission-Based Models

For High-Net-Worth-Individuals (HNIs) and Ultra-High-Net-Worth-Individuals (Ultra HNIs) seeking wealth management services, the advisory model is generally better suited compared to the commission-based model. The advisory model operates on a fee-based structure, where advisors charge a percentage of assets under management or a flat fee for their services. This aligns the advisor's interests with those of the client, fostering a more transparent and trust-based relationship. Advisors in this model are incentivized to focus on long-term financial planning, risk management, and personalized investment strategies tailored to the client's goals and risk tolerance. In contrast, the commission-based model may lead to potential conflicts of interest, as advisors earn commissions from selling financial products, which might not always align with the client's best interests. HNIs and Ultra HNIs typically prefer the advisory model for its emphasis on fiduciary responsibility, comprehensive financial planning, and the absence of product sales bias, ensuring that their wealth management needs are met with the highest level of integrity and expertise.

Karthik Athreya: In the context of advisory versus commission-based models, which approach do you believe is better suited for HNIs and Ultra HNIs seeking wealth management services?

Anupam Guha: The choice between advisory and commission-based models in wealth management hinges on transparency, alignment of interests, and value delivery. While both models have their merits, the advisory approach is increasingly favored by discerning HNIs and Ultra HNIs due to its emphasis on transparency, fee disclosure, and conflict-free advice. Under the advisory model, wealth managers act as fiduciaries, placing clients' interests paramount and providing personalized, unbiased advice tailored to their unique financial goals and risk profiles.

Conversely, commission-based models may introduce conflicts of interest, as wealth managers receive compensation based on product sales or transactions, potentially compromising the integrity of investment recommendations. As accredited investors prioritize transparency, value, and personalized service, the advisory model emerges as the preferred choice for wealth management, building trust, accountability, and long-term client relationships based on mutual respect and shared financial objectives.

Key Takeaways

- **Enhanced Client Relationships through Technology:** Technology empowers relationship managers with advanced tools and insights, leading to more personalized and effective client interactions and better decision-making.
- **Adoption of Technology:** Comprehensive training and ongoing support are essential for relationship managers to confidently embrace technology, transitioning from initial apprehension to improved efficiency and acceptance.
- **Strategic Leverage for Wealth Generation:** Leverage can enhance returns but also increase risks. Accredited investors must use leverage thoughtfully, balancing potential rewards with associated risks to improve portfolio performance.
- **Risk Management in Leveraged Investments:** Proper risk management strategies, such as diversification and setting clear risk limits, are critical to managing the complexities and potential downsides of leveraged investments.
- **Addressing Technological Threats:** Implementing up-to-date cybersecurity measures and proactive risk management practices is crucial for safeguarding clients' assets against cyber threats.
- **Advisory vs. Commission-Based Models:** The advisory model is preferred by HNIs and Ultra HNIs for its transparency, unbiased advice, and personalized service, ensuring alignment with clients' financial goals and preferences.

Chapter 08

Wealth and Asset Management: Contemporary Perspectives[8]

- This chapter examines wealth and asset management, highlighting the strategic use of technology, leveraging opportunities, and staying competitive. It focuses on adaptability, innovation, and aligning interests among stakeholders for long-term success.

- Guest Speaker: Mr. Karan Bhagat, Founder, MD, and CEO of 360 ONE.

  Mr. Bhagat has made significant strides in the industry since establishing the company in 2008. Under his astute leadership, 360 ONE boasts a team of over 1,000 professionals who cater to the needs of more than 6,800 top families in India. From its humble beginnings, 360 ONE has emerged as a leading wealth management company, overseeing approximately ₹383 crores in client assets.

- Speaker: Mr. Madanagopal Ramu, Head of Equity and Fund Manager at Sundaram Alternate Assets Ltd.

  With over 18 years of experience in the Indian Financial Markets, Mr. Madanagopal Ramu currently manages Assets Under Management (AUM) of around Rs. 3500 crores and has over 8 years of experience in managing funds. He manages

---

8   This chapter is based on The Alternates Universe episode shot on 25-08-23.

Sundaram India Secular Opportunities Portfolio (SISOP), Sundaram Emerging Leadership Fund (S.E.L.F.) and Voyager PMS strategies which have won awards at PMS Bazaar's PMS Rankings FY 21-22 event.

Foreword

At 360 ONE, we have built a distinctive place in the financial world, managing over U.S.$ 63 billion in client assets and guiding more than 7,400 HNI and Ultra HNI families in preserving and growing their wealth. Our reach extends to sovereign institutions and university endowments across the U.S., Canada, and the Middle East, a testament to our global expertise and trust.

From my early days in a travel agency, I have relied on adaptability and resilience to guide my career. As the Founder, MD & CEO of 360 ONE, I have the privilege and responsibility of steering our strategic direction, ensuring that our organization's goals align with our clients' evolving needs. From 360 ONE's inception in 2008, our guiding principle has been "Performance Plus."

360 ONE Asset has played a pivotal role in the growth of the Alternative Investment Fund (AIF) industry in India, offering a wide range of products, including AIFs, Portfolio Management Services (PMS), and mutual funds. Spanning public and private equity, fixed income, and real assets, these products are meticulously crafted to meet the sophisticated needs of our investors. Through innovation, we have consistently pushed the boundaries of what is possible in the investment landscape, exemplified by our industry-leading pre-IPO fund.

The Alternates Universe is a reflection of this dynamic and evolving world of alternate investments. The book serves not only as a chronicle of the past but also as a vision for the future, encouraging readers to explore the boundless opportunities within the alternate space. It brings together diverse viewpoints, demystifying complex strategies and highlighting the importance of aligning client interests with innovative investment approaches.

Throughout our journey, we have embraced the belief that challenging times often uncover the greatest opportunities. Resilience and innovation have been at the heart of our philosophy, and this has been particularly true in the world of alternative investments, where the ability to adapt and explore new horizons can lead to exceptional results. The Alternates Universe provides invaluable insights into this space, presenting a forum for top professionals to share their experiences, ideas, and strategies.

As we look to the future, discussions around sustainability, global economic shifts, and the evolving landscape of wealth management will continue to shape our industry. The Alternates Universe serves as an essential resource for those seeking to stay ahead of these trends, offering fresh perspectives and practical knowledge.

This book is more than a reflection on the past; it is a roadmap for navigating the complexities of tomorrow's financial landscape. I extend my gratitude to the creators of The Alternates Universe for offering a platform that not only educates but also inspires a new generation of wealth managers and investors. Together, we will continue to explore, innovate, and thrive in this ever-expanding universe of opportunities.

The Person Behind the Professional

Mr. Karan Bhagat's entrepreneurial journey commenced with the establishment of his own travel agency in Kolkata at the age of 17. While this phase of his life has been well-documented, what truly adds depth to his character is his multifaceted nature. Although he doesn't see himself as sales-oriented, his friends and colleagues disagree. They perceive him as the life of every gathering, someone who relishes meeting new people. Colleagues describe him as trustworthy, always supportive, and a dedicated workaholic. However, the most recurrent descriptor of Mr. Bhagat is his remarkable humility, which defines him both personally and professionally.

Interactions with Mr. Bhagat reveal an individual who values open communication and empowerment. He has developed an environment where ideas are freely exchanged without fear of judgment, yet he can be hands-on when necessary. Thorough research and industry insights inform his viewpoints, and he gracefully accepts counterarguments supported by data and logic. Beyond his professional persona, Mr. Bhagat is an avid reader of classics like "The Intelligent Investor" but stays current by engaging with people from diverse backgrounds. He is known for his confidence in execution over mere imagination, and he doesn't hesitate to express his ideas publicly. Despite his chilled-out demeanor, he becomes impassioned when he perceives a lack of effort or integrity in others.

On a personal level, Mr. Bhagat finds comfort in casual attire and cherishes family time. He is a proud father to twins, who excel in judo and academics, respectively. His wife, Shilpa, is an influencer and fitness enthusiast who is actively involved in various pursuits. While Mr. Bhagat enjoys beach vacations and indulges in sports like tennis and cricket, his Kolkata roots shine through his love for street food. Furthermore, Mr. Bhagat is deeply committed to community service, particularly in promoting sports and education. He supports chess tournaments nationwide and champions initiatives for children's education. Through his multifaceted endeavors, Mr. Karan Bhagat embodies humility, dedication, and a genuine commitment to making a positive impact in both his professional and personal spheres.

Introduction

Wealth and asset management strategies are evolving, blending traditional approaches with innovative techniques to tackle the complexities of the financial landscape. Investors now combine smart asset allocation, momentum investing, and dollar-cost averaging to enhance returns and manage risks. The growing prominence of private equity and real estate is reshaping portfolios, while technological advancements like automated trading systems and blockchain are making investment decisions more intelligent. Additionally, the emphasis on sustainable and ethical investing aligns financial goals with personal values. As these strategies continue to adapt to global economic shifts and events, staying flexible and well-informed is crucial for seizing opportunities and effectively managing risks.

Adversity and Opportunity

Vikaas M Sachdeva: You've emphasized how adversity often presents the best opportunities. Can you elaborate on how facing adversity has led to significant opportunities in your life and career?

Karan Bhagat: Certainly, adversity has been a catalyst for many opportunities in my journey. When my father's business faced challenges during the Asian currency crisis, I started my own travel agency, gaining invaluable experience in sales and negotiation. This taught me resilience and resourcefulness, which have been instrumental in subsequent endeavors.

Career Transitions

Vikaas M Sachdeva: Your journey has been marked by significant transitions, such as starting your own business and transitioning to different roles. How have you managed these transitions effectively, especially during times of uncertainty like the 2001 financial downturn?

Karan Bhagat: Transitioning between different phases of my career has been challenging yet rewarding. The 2001 financial downturn taught me the importance of adaptability. Joining Kotak Securities during unexpected layoffs opened doors to new experiences. Remaining open to change, focusing on learning and growth, and being resilient have been key.

Balancing Earnings and Profitability

Vikaas M Sachdeva: Could you elaborate on the insights you gained regarding the balance between individual earnings and firm profitability?

Karan Bhagat: Understanding revenue generation and firm profitability has been crucial. Individual earnings are tied to the firm's success. Contributing to the firm's success through effective client service, innovation, and collaboration creates a win-win situation for both employees and the organization.

Maintaining a Competitive Edge

Maintaining a competitive edge in a challenging market requires a strategic focus on people, platforms, and products. Investing in a skilled and motivated workforce ensures that the organization benefits from innovative ideas and exceptional service delivery. Providing continuous training and fostering a culture of collaboration and excellence can significantly enhance performance. Leveraging advanced technology platforms is crucial for streamlining operations, improving customer experiences, and enabling data-driven decision-making. These platforms should be scalable and adaptable to evolving market demands. Additionally, offering a diverse and high-quality product portfolio that meets the changing needs and preferences of customers is essential. Regularly updating and innovating products based on market research and feedback ensures relevance and competitiveness. By integrating these elements—talented people, cutting-edge platforms, and superior products—organizations can effectively navigate market challenges and achieve sustained success.

Madanagopal Ramu: How do you maintain a competitive edge in a challenging market, especially considering the multiplying effect of people, platforms, and products on success?

Karan Bhagat: Maintaining a competitive edge requires focusing on people, platforms, and products. Investing in talent and promoting a culture of innovation ensures we have the best people driving our success. Enhancing our platform and technology infrastructure allows us to deliver superior service. Offering innovative products and staying ahead of market trends to meet evolving client needs.

Aligning Interests of Stakeholders

Aligning the interests of stakeholders is essential for the success and sustainability of any organization. Stakeholders, including employees, customers, investors, suppliers, and the community, each have unique priorities and expectations. To achieve alignment, organizations must engage in active communication and collaboration, ensuring that all parties understand the company's goals and how they can contribute to achieving them. This often involves negotiating compromises and finding common ground where the interests of different stakeholders intersect. For example, ensuring fair labor practices can enhance employee satisfaction, which in turn can improve customer service and ultimately benefit investors through increased profitability. Transparent reporting and regular updates can help build trust and demonstrate commitment to stakeholder interests. By aligning these diverse interests, organizations can create a cohesive strategy that supports long-term growth and positive relationships with all stakeholders.

Madanagopal Ramu: Can you share strategies that have helped you maintain alignment and positive relationships among stakeholders?

Karan Bhagat: Aligning stakeholder interests is important. Encouraging open communication and transparency across all levels of the organization creates a shared vision. Incentivizing behaviors that promote collaboration and client satisfaction further reinforce alignment and positive relationships among stakeholders.

The Power of Compounding

Compounding is a key financial principle where returns generate additional earnings, which are reinvested to create even more growth. This snowball effect accelerates over time, making early and consistent investments especially powerful. The longer the investment period, the greater the potential for significant growth, even from small contributions. It is vital for long-term goals like retirement, showing the value of patience and steady saving to build wealth.

Madanagopal Ramu: How do you approach long-term growth and sustainability, especially as you transition from one phase to the next?

Karan Bhagat: The power of compounding is fundamental. Strategic investments in talent, technology, and innovation drive future success. Maintaining a disciplined approach to risk management and capital allocation ensures we can weather challenges and seize opportunities. Staying true to our core values and long-term vision creates enduring value for all stakeholders.

Vision Behind Entrepreneurship

Vikaas M Sachdeva: Could you share the vision behind your journey into entrepreneurship and the inception of your business?

Karan Bhagat: My journey into entrepreneurship wasn't initially driven by a grand vision. In 2006, a suggestion to explore setting up a family office intrigued me. Understanding family offices during Bank of America Merrill Lynch's transition to advisory services emphasized reducing friction in client relationships. Despite challenges, this client-centric approach was pivotal.

Promoting a Culture of Innovation

Promoting a culture of innovation within an organization involves creating an environment where creativity and new ideas are encouraged and valued. This starts with leadership that is open to change and willing to take calculated risks. Encouraging open communication and collaboration across all levels of the organization can help generate diverse perspectives and ideas. Providing employees with the resources and time to explore new concepts is also essential, as is recognizing and rewarding innovative efforts. Additionally, embracing failure as a learning opportunity rather than a setback can motivate employees to experiment without fear of repercussions. By embedding innovation into the company's values and everyday practices, organizations can continuously adapt and improve, staying competitive in a rapidly changing market.

Vikaas M Sachdeva: How do you encourage a culture of innovation within your organization?

Karan Bhagat: Innovation is more about culture than isolated ideas. During our early days, we innovated in small but impactful ways, like tweaking fee structures for structured products. Collective brainstorming and a willingness to optimize even the smallest details continually drive our innovation.

Future Trends in Alternative Investments

The alternative investment space is expected to be shaped by several key trends in the coming years, including increased interest in sustainable and impact investing, the rise of digital assets, and greater regulatory scrutiny. Sustainable and impact investing will continue to gain traction as investors seek to align their portfolios with environmental, social, and governance (ESG) criteria. The growing popularity of digital assets, such as cryptocurrencies and blockchain-based investments, will attract tech-savvy investors looking for high returns and diversification. Additionally, regulatory bodies are likely to impose stricter guidelines to ensure transparency and protect investors. To adapt, firms should enhance their expertise in ESG and digital assets, invest in advanced analytics and compliance technologies, and offer tailored products that meet evolving investor preferences. By staying ahead of these trends, firms can attract and retain clients while navigating the complexities of the alternative investment landscape.

Vikaas M Sachdeva: What trends do you foresee shaping the alternative investment space in the next few years, and how should firms adapt?

Karan Bhagat: Alternative investments span various categories globally. In India, credit is poised for significant growth post-regulatory changes. Yield assets like REITs and InvITs hold promise, though tax structures might hinder long-short strategies. Firms should anticipate these shifts and align their offerings accordingly.

Exiting Investments

Several red flags may signal that it is time to exit a mutual fund or investment strategy. Consistently underperforming benchmarks is a significant indicator, suggesting that the fund is not meeting its investment objectives. High turnover in the fund's management team can also be a concern, as it may lead to inconsistent investment approaches and strategies. Increasing expense ratios without corresponding performance improvements can erode returns, making the investment less attractive. Additionally, significant changes in the fund's investment strategy or asset allocation that do not align with your financial goals or risk tolerance are warning signs. Poor transparency and communication from the fund management about performance and strategy changes can also undermine confidence. Lastly, broader market conditions or personal financial needs may necessitate re-evaluating and potentially exiting the investment. Monitoring these factors can help investors make informed decisions about when to exit a mutual fund or investment strategy.

Vikaas M Sachdeva: What are some red flags signaling it might be time to exit a mutual fund or investment strategy?

Karan Bhagat: Key indicators include excessive fund size, inconsistent performance, and evolving market dynamics. Oversized funds struggle with liquidity constraints. Erratic performance or deviation from the investment strategy warrants caution. Evolving market dynamics require reassessing holdings to ensure alignment with financial goals.

Growth vs. Boutique Approach

Choosing between a growth-oriented approach and a boutique approach in business strategy depends on the specific goals and resources of the firm. A growth-oriented approach focuses on scaling operations, expanding market reach, and increasing revenue through aggressive marketing, product diversification, and mergers or acquisitions. This strategy aims to capture a larger market share and achieve economies of scale. In contrast, a boutique approach emphasizes specialized services, personalized client relationships, and niche market expertise. Firms adopting this strategy prioritize quality over quantity, offering tailored solutions and a high level of customer service to differentiate themselves from larger competitors. While growth strategies can lead to rapid expansion and higher market visibility, boutique firms can build strong, loyal client bases by delivering exceptional value and expertise. The choice between these approaches should align with the firm's long-term vision, market conditions, and core competencies.

Vikaas M Sachdeva: For midsize wealth management firms, would you advise focusing on further growth or maintaining a boutique approach? What are the challenges in retaining AUM (Assets Under Management)?

Karan Bhagat: Midsize firms must balance growth aspirations with operational sustainability. Scaling enhances competitiveness, but maintaining boutique service standards is crucial. Ensuring robust cash flows and optimizing scale is paramount. To retain AUM, firms should prioritize client education and align investment decisions with client objectives. Understanding intergenerational wealth transitions is vital for AUM retention.

Key Takeaways

- **Turning Adversity into Opportunity:** Adversity often opens doors to new opportunities. Experiences such as starting a business during challenging times can lead to the development of resilience and resourcefulness, crucial traits for long-term success.

- **Managing Career Transitions:** Navigating significant career changes, especially during uncertain times, requires flexibility, a commitment to learning, and an openness to new experiences. These qualities help in adapting to new roles and seizing unexpected opportunities.

- **Balancing Personal Earnings with Firm Success:** Understanding the interplay between personal earnings and firm profitability is key. When individual contributions align with the firm's overall success, both the employee and the organization benefit, creating a mutually rewarding environment.

- **Staying Competitive in a Challenging Market:** Maintaining a competitive edge involves a strategic focus on enhancing human capital, utilizing advanced technology platforms, and continuously innovating product offerings to meet the evolving needs of clients. This approach helps organizations stay relevant and effective.

- **Aligning Stakeholder Interests:** Ensuring that the interests of all stakeholders—employees, clients, investors, and the community—are aligned is vital. Open communication and transparency across all levels of the organization help build trust and promote collaboration, leading to stronger and more cohesive relationships.

- **Harnessing the Power of Compounding:** Compounding is a powerful tool in wealth generation. By making strategic, long-term investments and managing risks carefully, it's possible to achieve significant growth over time, emphasizing the importance of patience and disciplined financial planning.

- **Encouraging a Culture of Innovation:** Innovation thrives in an environment where creativity is encouraged and where even small, incremental improvements are valued. Leadership that supports and rewards innovative thinking can help an organization continuously adapt and improve, staying ahead in a competitive market.

- **Adapting to Emerging Investment Trends:** The investment environment is constantly shifting, with new trends such as sustainable investing, digital assets, and regulatory changes coming to the forefront. Firms need to anticipate these trends and adjust their strategies accordingly to stay competitive and meet the evolving demands of investors.

- **Identifying the Right Time to Exit Investments:** Regularly assessing the performance of investments and staying aware of market dynamics is crucial. Signs like inconsistent returns, changes in strategy, or shifts in the broader market environment can indicate when it's time to exit an investment.

- **Balancing Growth with a Boutique Approach:** For midsize firms, the challenge is balancing the desire for growth with the need to maintain the personalized service that clients expect from a boutique firm. Understanding and managing the nuances of intergenerational wealth transitions is also crucial for retaining Assets Under Management (AUM).

Chapter 09

Current Landscape of Equity Markets: Key Opportunities[9]

- This chapter explores the opportunities in the current equity market scenario, focusing on technological advancements, strategic leverage, and global diversification to enhance wealth generation.

- Guest Speaker: Mr. Ashish Shanker, Managing Director and Chief Executive Officer, Motilal Oswal Private Wealth.

  As the architect of the investment platform at Motilal Oswal Private Wealth, Mr. Shanker has garnered recognition for pioneering initiatives such as the highly acclaimed 4C framework for selecting fund managers and the innovative Delphi platform solutions.

- Speaker: Mr. Karthik Athreya, Head – Fund Strategy (Private Credit) at Sundaram Alternates.

  Mr. Karthik Athreya is a financial services professional with over 22 years of experience across principal investing, funds management, investment banking, corporate finance, assurance, and transaction diligence services. He heads Sundaram Alternates' (SAA) private credit team, which manages assets of over USD 275 million in a short span of 5 years across real estate and private credit.

---

9   This chapter is based on The Alternates Universe episode shot on 22-09-23.

The Person Behind the Professional

His colleagues and friends widely regard Mr. Ashish Shanker as approachable and congenial. Renowned for his collaborative nature, he encourages an environment of camaraderie and teamwork, eschewing hierarchical dynamics. A voracious reader with a keen interest in finance, economics, and business, Mr. Shanker draws inspiration from renowned authors like Michael Mauboussin, whose insights have profoundly influenced his approach to financial strategies. As the editor of Alpha Strategist, a prestigious financial publication, he demonstrates a commitment to disseminating knowledge and shaping discourse within the industry, earning accolades from peers and admirers alike.

In addition to his intellectual pursuits, Mr. Shanker exhibits a competitive spirit and a penchant for precision in his professional endeavors. Leading from the front in business dealings, he maintains a composed demeanor while striving for excellence in every task. His meticulous attention to detail, particularly in financial matters, commands respect from colleagues, who are acutely aware of his ability to discern errors with remarkable acuity. While his directives may appear formal and conventional, Mr. Shanker's dedication to quality and diligence underscores his unwavering standards of professionalism.

Beyond the confines of the corporate world, Mr. Shanker leads a multifaceted life enriched by diverse interests and passions. A devoted family man with a penchant for sports, he shares a deep love for football with his son, having traveled together to witness the excitement of the FIFA World Cup. Despite his professional achievements, Mr. Shanker remains grounded, finding joy in simple pleasures such as exploring new culinary experiences and sharing laughter with friends. Embodying the wisdom imparted by a mentor, he embraces equanimity in handling life's challenges, maintaining a sense of humor and humility amidst triumphs and setbacks.

Introduction

Navigating the current equity market scenario demands a blend of traditional wisdom and innovative strategies to uncover new opportunities and manage risks effectively. Investors are increasingly adopting approaches like strategic asset allocation, momentum investing, and dollar-cost averaging to optimize returns. The rise of private equity and real estate investments is transforming portfolio structures, while advancements in technology, such as automated trading systems and blockchain, are enhancing decision-making processes. Additionally, the growing focus on sustainable and ethical investing allows investors to align their financial goals with personal values. As these strategies evolve in response to global economic changes, maintaining flexibility and staying well-informed are crucial for capitalizing on market opportunities and mitigating risks.

Market Insights and Trends

The Indian economy had shown significant resilience and growth, closing 2023 with a GDP of $3.73 trillion and a per capita income of $2,610. Key sectors such as manufacturing, infrastructure, and real estate exhibited robust performance, supported by government initiatives like the 'Make in India' campaign and the Production-Linked Incentive (PLI) scheme. Despite global economic challenges, India's GDP growth was projected at 6.3%, well above the global average. Consumer behavior shifted towards a preference for authenticity and local identities in media and entertainment. The financial markets saw strong inflows from both domestic and foreign investors, though there were concerns about rising household debt and inflation. The stock market experienced modest growth, with the Nifty 50 index reaching new highs. Overall, India's strategic focus on infrastructure development, technology investment, and expanding consumer markets positioned it for continued growth and stability.

Vikaas M Sachdeva: With the markets at an all-time high or near it, what's in store for the Indian stock markets? Are we due for a pause or a correction?

Ashish Shanker: Absolutely. This is indeed a pertinent question that's on everyone's mind. Howard Knox's perspective on market cycles resonates strongly here. Currently, we find ourselves in a phase that's quite favorable for the Indian economy and its equity markets. The last decade wasn't particularly stellar for Indian stocks, but now we're seeing a shift. Solid economic fundamentals and corporate profitability back the current rally.

For instance, while the Nifty index hasn't seen significant gains in recent years, earnings have surged by about 30%. This disparity indicates that markets are actually cheaper now compared to two years ago. With earnings visibility promising for the next few years, we're confidently in a bull market phase. So, rather than predicting short-term fluctuations, the focus should be on the broader trajectory, which appears optimistic for the next three to five years. Thus, longer-term investors may perceive corrections as buying opportunities akin to previous bull market cycles.

Vikaas M Sachdeva: That's a comprehensive analysis indeed. Shifting gears slightly, what are the three trends you foresee emerging over the next three years, particularly from a medium-term perspective?

Ashish Shanker: Certainly, Mr. Sachdeva. Looking ahead, several trends are poised to shape the investment environment. Firstly, investment-related themes are likely to thrive as India witnesses increased infrastructure development and private sector capex. Government initiatives in sectors like roads and defense, coupled with private capex driven by improving demand visibility, indicate substantial growth potential.

Additionally, the "China plus one" manufacturing trend and rising domestic demand are bolstering sectors like steel and chemicals. Secondly, as India's per capita income rises, there'll be a surge in demand for discretionary categories like apparel, automobiles, and housing, creating what I term a "demand storm." This transition from a

$2,500 to a $4,000 per capita income bracket will significantly impact consumption patterns. Lastly, with globalization accelerating, investors are increasingly eyeing global markets for diversification and higher returns. While Indian assets will remain integral to portfolios, allocating funds to established markets like the U.S. offers both diversification benefits and potential currency gains.

Global Integration and Portfolio Diversification

When investing in emerging markets, investors must consider the risks and benefits of market volatility and currency fluctuations. Rupee-denominated portfolios can be advantageous for Indian investors as they avoid the currency risk associated with foreign investments. However, the Indian rupee has historically depreciated against the U.S. dollar, which can erode returns when converting to other currencies. On the other hand, dollar-denominated portfolios offer diversification and the potential for higher returns. Nonetheless, these portfolios are subject to currency risk, where unfavorable exchange rate movements can impact returns. Emerging markets, including India, often face higher volatility, political instability, and liquidity issues, which can further complicate investment decisions. Ultimately, a balanced approach that includes both rupee and dollar-denominated assets can help mitigate risks and capitalize on growth opportunities across different markets.

Karthik Athreya: Speaking of global integration, how do you view the debate between building rupee versus dollar-denominated portfolios, considering emerging market risks and currency volatility?

Ashish Shanker: Integrating with the global economy is vital, given the aspirations of affluent Indians and the prevalence of digital content consumption. While Indian assets will remain a core part of portfolios, there's growing interest in diversifying into dollar-denominated assets for additional risk mitigation and exposure to global growth drivers. The U.S. market, in particular, offers diversification benefits due to its lower correlation with Indian equities and potential currency gains during rupee depreciation. While navigating this transition, investors should adopt a gradual approach, starting with U.S. index funds and gradually expanding exposure based on their risk tolerance and investment goals.

Opportunities for Alpha Generation

There are many opportunities to generate alpha across different sectors. Investors have found promising prospects in new-age technology stocks, private financials, and undervalued traditional tech companies. The "China plus one" strategy has also opened up avenues in sectors like specialty chemicals and manufacturing. With over 6,000 listed companies and a vibrant IPO market, India presents a fertile ground for stock-specific investments. The country's robust economic growth, coupled with government initiatives, has further bolstered investor confidence. By strategically allocating capital to high-growth sectors and leveraging market-specific opportunities, investors can achieve substantial excess returns, or alpha, in the Indian market.

Karthik Athreya: Your insights are invaluable. Moving beyond traditional equity investments, what other opportunities do you see for alpha generation among Ultra HNIs or family offices?

Ashish Shanker: Certainly, Mr. Athreya. Beyond equities, several avenues offer potential for alpha generation. Structured credit funds present opportunities for high yields through deals with corporations with strong cash flows. Similarly, real estate funds leverage structured credit with real estate collateral, offering attractive risk-adjusted returns.

Additionally, global bonds provide opportunities for stable returns and currency diversification, especially amidst favorable global bond yields. Innovative financial products like retail REITs offer a blend of equity upside and predictable cash flows. With increasing capital formation and innovative investment products, the environment for alpha generation is changing rapidly.

The Growing Demand for Private Credit

The demand for private credit in India has surged significantly, driven by several factors, including the tightening of traditional bank lending and the need for alternative financing solutions. In 2023, private credit deals saw a nearly 47% increase in value, reaching $7.8 billion, as traditional lenders faced challenges such as the NBFC crisis and growing NPAs. Private credit funds have stepped in to fill this gap, offering tailored solutions to higher-risk borrowers, such as SMEs and real estate firms, who struggle to access conventional bank loans. This growth has been supported by regulatory developments like the Insolvency and Bankruptcy Code, which has improved recovery processes. With high returns attracting both domestic and foreign investors, private credit is poised to play a crucial role in India's financial ecosystem, providing much-needed capital to underserved sectors and driving economic growth.

Vikaas M Sachdeva: I recently made a presentation on the demand for private credit, which has seen a significant uptick. We've noticed that about 30 percent of the capital requirements for unlisted companies or unicorns will be met through private credit in the next three years. This includes the growing category of venture debt. What are your thoughts on this trend?

Ashish Shanker: The surge in demand for private credit, especially among unlisted companies and unicorns, signals a notable shift in the financing sector. With approximately 30 percent of the capital requirements for these entities expected to be met through private credit over the next three years, this trend underscores the growing importance of alternative financing sources. Venture debt, in particular, has emerged as a significant contributor to meeting the funding needs of such enterprises. As traditional financing avenues may not always adequately address the capital requirements of rapidly growing and innovative businesses, private credit strategies offer tailored solutions to support their expansion and development efforts.

Our firm's experience and observations corroborate the increasing relevance of private credit strategies in meeting the capital needs of unlisted companies and unicorns. The ability to access flexible financing options through private credit instruments allows these entities to fuel their growth initiatives while maintaining operational agility. As highlighted in our recent presentation, the dynamics driving this trend are multifaceted, encompassing factors such as changing market conditions, the regulatory environment, and the unique financing needs of emerging businesses. By embracing private credit solutions, companies can capitalize on opportunities for expansion and innovation while mitigating the constraints associated with traditional lending channels.

The growing demand for private credit, including venture debt, reflects a strategic shift in the financing preferences of unlisted companies and unicorns. As these entities seek tailored financing solutions to support their growth trajectories, private credit strategies offer a compelling alternative to traditional funding avenues. By leveraging the flexibility and agility inherent in private credit instruments, businesses can access the capital needed to pursue their strategic objectives while navigating the evolving scenarios of today's financial markets.

The 4C Framework for Evaluating Fund Strategies

The 4C framework is a strategic tool used to evaluate fund strategies by examining four key elements: Customer, Competition, Cost, and Capabilities. In the Indian context, this framework helps investors and fund managers gain a comprehensive understanding of the market and make informed decisions. Customer analysis focuses on understanding the needs and behaviors of different investor segments, including retail and institutional investors. Competition involves assessing the market position and strategies of competing funds to identify differentiation opportunities. Cost analysis looks at the cost structure of the fund, including management fees and operational expenses, to ensure competitive pricing and profitability. Finally, Capabilities examines the fund's internal strengths, such as investment expertise, technology, and human resources, to determine its ability to execute strategies effectively. By systematically analyzing these four areas, fund managers can develop robust strategies that align with market conditions and investor expectations.

Vikaas M Sachdeva: Now, turning to your role as an Alpha Strategist, I've noticed your well-respected 4C framework in evaluating fund strategies. For the benefit of our audience, could you explain how you select and recommend fund strategies using this framework?

Ashish Shanker: Certainly, the 4C framework, influenced by the writings of Michael Mauboussin, is a cornerstone of our evaluation process. Firstly, we focus on the clarity of the fund manager's philosophy. Understanding their investment approach, whether it's value-oriented, growth-oriented, or another style, is key. Consistency in applying this philosophy is equally important. We analyze past performance trends to gauge this.

Secondly, we assess the fund manager's capabilities, including their team structure and expertise. Thirdly, we consider the fund manager's track record across market cycles, ensuring they have navigated various market conditions competently. Lastly, we evaluate the fund manager's experience, referring to their background in managing different asset classes and market environments.

The Role of Gold in Diversification

Gold plays a pivotal role in diversification, particularly in the Indian context, where it is both a cultural asset and a financial instrument. As a hedge against inflation and currency fluctuations, gold provides stability in times of economic uncertainty. Its low correlation with other asset classes like equities and bonds makes it an effective tool for risk management. During market downturns, gold often retains or even increases in value, offering a safety net for investors. In India, where gold is traditionally favored for both investment and jewelry, incorporating gold into a diversified portfolio can help balance risk and enhance long-term returns. Whether through physical gold, ETFs, or sovereign gold bonds, this precious metal remains a trusted component for achieving financial resilience.

Vikaas M Sachdeva: Moving on to another topic, many investors are curious about the role of gold in diversification. What's your take on the ideal allocation of gold within a diversified portfolio?

Ashish Shanker: Gold plays a significant role in diversification due to its unique properties as a hedge against market downturns and economic uncertainties. During times of crisis, such as market crashes or geopolitical instability, gold tends to maintain or increase in value, acting as a safe haven for investors. Therefore, allocating a portion of a diversified portfolio to gold, typically between 10-20 percent, provides a buffer against the volatility and downside risks associated with equities and other assets. This allocation strategy aims to preserve capital and stabilize portfolio returns during turbulent market conditions.

The recommended allocation to gold within a diversified portfolio serves to mitigate risk and enhance overall portfolio performance. By spreading investment across multiple asset classes, including gold, investors can reduce correlation and increase diversification benefits. Gold's historical track record of preserving wealth over the long-term further supports its role as a strategic asset allocation. Regular rebalancing of the gold allocation, typically on an annual basis, helps maintain the desired risk-return profile of the portfolio, ensuring it remains aligned with the investor's objectives and risk tolerance.

In summary, the ideal allocation of gold within a diversified portfolio is designed to provide downside protection and enhance risk-adjusted returns. By allocating a portion of the portfolio to gold, investors can benefit from its diversification properties and resilience during market downturns. This strategic allocation, coupled with periodic rebalancing, enables investors to navigate through various market conditions while preserving capital and achieving long-term investment objectives.

Expected Returns and Asset Allocation

Expected returns and asset allocation are fundamental concepts in investment strategy, especially in the Indian context. For 2023, equities in India are projected to offer attractive returns, driven by robust economic growth and strong corporate earnings. Fixed-income investments, while providing lower returns compared to equities, offer stability and regular income, making them a vital component of a balanced portfolio. Gold continues to be a safe haven, providing a hedge against inflation and currency volatility, and is expected to maintain its value amidst economic uncertainties. Real estate, with its potential for capital appreciation and rental income, remains a popular choice for long-term investors. Effective asset allocation involves diversifying investments across these asset classes to optimize returns while managing risk. By balancing high-growth equities, stable fixed income, resilient gold, and appreciating real estate, investors can achieve a well-rounded portfolio tailored to their risk tolerance and financial goals.

Vikaas M Sachdeva: That's a clear and actionable recommendation, Ashish. Now, let's address another audience query regarding the expected returns on different market segments. How do you view the distribution of investments across large, mid, and small-cap companies to achieve a targeted return on capital?

Ashish Shanker: Returns on capital vary across market segments, but we aim for a comprehensive approach. Typically, we expect around 12 percent returns on equities, factoring in inflation rates. Regarding allocation, we suggest a blend of large, mid, and small-cap companies, with larger allocations to large caps for stability. However, specific market conditions may influence these allocations.

Real Estate Investment Outlook

The outlook for real estate investment in India remains highly promising as we move into 2024. The sector has shown remarkable resilience and growth, with the market size reaching $265.18 billion in 2023, up by 32% since 2021. Residential sales have hit a 15-year high, driven by strong consumer demand and favorable economic conditions. Infrastructure developments, such as the upcoming Noida International Airport and various connectivity projects in Navi Mumbai, are expected to further boost real estate activity in surrounding areas. Additionally, the commercial real estate segment continues to grow, supported by increasing demand for tech-enabled office spaces. Regulatory reforms, such as the introduction of Small and Medium REITs (SM REITs), have also made it easier for investors to enter the market. With a projected compound annual growth rate (CAGR) of 9.2% from 2023 to 2028, the Indian real estate sector is poised for sustained expansion, offering lucrative opportunities for both domestic and international investors.

Vikaas M Sachdeva: Lastly, let's discuss real estate, which remains a significant investment avenue. Do you anticipate further growth in the sector, considering current market dynamics?

Ashish Shanker: Real estate's outlook depends on several factors, including market volumes and pricing trends. While volumes have surged recently, pricing remains relatively stable. Affordability indices suggest that real estate values are reasonable, presenting opportunities for both investors and end-users. However, market conditions vary across regions, requiring careful analysis before making investment decisions.

Key Takeaways

- **India's Economic Growth and Market Potential:** India's economy is poised for continued growth, driven by solid economic fundamentals, corporate profitability, and strategic government initiatives. This presents a favorable environment for long-term equity investments, especially in sectors like infrastructure, manufacturing, and real estate.

- **The Role of Corporate Earnings in Market Valuation:** Despite recent modest gains in market indices, corporate earnings have surged by approximately 30%, indicating that Indian markets are more attractively valued now than in previous years. Long-term investors may view potential market corrections as buying opportunities.

- **Emerging Investment Themes:** Infrastructure development, rising private sector capital expenditure, and domestic demand will drive growth in key sectors like steel, chemicals, apparel, automobiles, and housing over the next few years. This "demand storm" is expected to reshape India's consumption landscape.

- **Global Diversification and Currency Considerations:** A balanced portfolio that includes both rupee and dollar-denominated assets can help investors mitigate risks related to market volatility and currency fluctuations. Diversifying into global markets, particularly the U.S., can provide opportunities for higher returns and currency gains.

- **Sector-Specific Alpha Generation:** High-growth opportunities in sectors like new-age technology, private financials, and traditional tech companies offer significant alpha potential. The "China plus one" strategy also creates investment opportunities in sectors like specialty chemicals and manufacturing.

- **Private Credit as an Alternative Investment Opportunity:** The demand for private credit is on the rise in India, especially among unlisted companies and unicorns. Private credit funds are stepping in to fill gaps left by traditional banks, offering flexible financing options and supporting capital needs in underserved sectors.

- **4C Framework for Evaluating Fund Strategies:** The 4C framework (Customer, Competition, Cost, and Capabilities) provides a comprehensive approach to evaluating fund strategies. It ensures that fund managers' philosophy, track record, team expertise, and cost structures are aligned with market conditions and investor expectations.

- **Gold as a Diversification Tool:** Gold continues to play a critical role in portfolio diversification, especially in the Indian market. It serves as a hedge against inflation and economic uncertainty, with an ideal allocation between 10-20% of a portfolio to stabilize returns during market downturns.

- **Expected Returns on Market Segments:** Returns on equities are projected to be around 12%, with large-cap companies offering stability while mid- and small-caps provide higher growth potential. Diversifying across these segments can optimize returns while managing risk.

- **Real Estate Investment Outlook:** The Indian real estate sector is expected to see continued growth, driven by infrastructure development, favorable economic conditions, and regulatory reforms. Investors should remain mindful of regional market dynamics when making real estate investment decisions.

Chapter 10

Family Offices Unveiled: Advanced Strategies[10]

- In this chapter, we explore the insights and experiences of leading experts in the field, shedding light on the evolving role of family offices in managing wealth, ensuring continuity, and navigating the complexities of global financial markets.

- Guest Speaker: Ms. Himanshu Kohli, Co-founder of Client Associates.

  Ms. Kohli brings over three decades of expertise in investment banking and private banking. As the co-founder of Client Associates, she has built a team of private bankers dedicated to serving wealthy families nationwide. Her experience includes significant tenures with Deutsche Bank Private Banking, DSP Merrill Lynch, and London Forfaiting Group.

- Speaker: Mr. Arjun G. Nagarajan, Commodities Fund Manager, Chief Economist and Communications Manager, Sundaram Asset Management Company

  Arjun G Nagarajan works at Sundaram Mutual as the Commodities Fund Manager. After spending 3 years in academics, Arjun built a career in the equity market spanning over 12 years, with more than 10 of those years being spent at Sundaram Mutual. Arjun was a part of the NITI Aayog's discussion with economists on topical issues in the recent past.

---

10 This chapter is based on The Alternates Universe episode shot on 29-12-23.

Foreword

Client Associates is India's largest Private Wealth Management and Multi-Family Office company, committed to assisting wealthy families in India and worldwide. We aim to become the most reliable and respected wealth management company in India, providing personalized financial services such as Investment Banking, Private Banking, and Estate Planning while upholding the values of Trust, Talent, and Transparency. The foundation of our company is centered around adding value through customized interactions and developing strong and significant connections with our customers. We serve as the personal Chief Financial Officer (CFO) for our clients, overseeing the finances of about 1200 HNI and UHNI families with a combined value of more than USD 6.2 billion. The central principle of "Client-Centricity" in our name demonstrates our dedication to prioritizing the interests of our clients.

I have been working in the industry for almost thirty years, with experience at renowned companies like Deutsche Bank Private Banking, DSP Merrill Lynch, and the London Forfaiting Group. This experience in 2002 paved the way for co-founding Client Associates and introducing the "Family Office" concept in India. Today, Client Associates is established as the first and biggest Multi-Family Office Firm in India, based on a philosophy that prioritizes the client. Our team of personal bankers is committed to empowering rich and prosperous families with careful wealth management and creative financial planning.

The Alternates Universe series is a significant effort for the wealth management and alternative industry. It offers a space for industry leaders to exchange their experiences, perspectives, and tactics. What impresses me about the program is its knack for connecting traditional and modern strategies in wealth management. By presenting varied outlooks on wealth management, addressing succession planning, and navigating intricate financial markets, it encapsulates the changing nature of our industry. The program stands out for its in-depth look at different management styles and its thorough examination of alternative investments.

During my involvement in the series, I have highlighted the need to maintain a well-rounded investment strategy. At Client Associates, we combine conventional investment strategies with alternative investments to maximize our clients' wealth and ensure their financial futures. The conversations in the series have strengthened my conviction in the importance of varied portfolios and robust risk management tactics, particularly as clients' assets exceed their current requirements.

The Alternates Universe series provides substantial value for wealth managers, investors, and the broader financial community. It reveals new tactics and enhances the comprehension of alternative investments, which are now a substantial part of HNI and UHNI portfolios. The series assists professionals in understanding the complexities of modern wealth management by emphasizing the importance of diversification and risk management, offering practical insights to optimize their investment strategies.

In the future, I am enthusiastic about the possibility of future editions of The Alternates Universe to dive deeper into new ideas and strategies in the wealth management sector. I hope season 2 will continue to present new viewpoints that can assist wealth managers in staying ahead of trends.

I urge readers to spare some time for this book and the abundance of information it provides. The shared interpretations will definitely inspire and educate, enhancing the development and achievement of our industry. I would like to thank the team who created The Alternates Universe for giving me this chance, and I am excited to keep working with them to improve the wealth management and alternatives sector.

The Person Behind the Professional

Mr. Himanshu Kohli's journey from DSP Merrill Lynch to founding Client Associates in Delhi reflects a remarkable blend of youthfulness and foresight. His transition from the corporate world to entrepreneurship marked a significant chapter in his career, laying the foundation for Client Associates' success. His vision and leadership have propelled the firm to establish itself as a gold standard in wealth management, which is evident in its growth trajectory and industry accolades. An openness to innovation and experimentation characterizes Mr. Kohli and his firm, exemplified by initiatives like the Experience Lounge in Kolkata. This commitment to embracing new ideas underscores Client Associates' reputation as a trailblazer in the wealth management landscape.

Beyond professional achievements, Mr. Kohli's team reveres him for his approachability, kindness, and patience. His dedication to clear communication and punctuality sets a high standard for professionalism within the organization. Passion for fitness and sports, coupled with meticulous attention to detail in both personal and professional domains, reflects Mr. Kohli's multifaceted personality. A devoted family man, Mr. Kohli celebrates 25 years of blissful marriage with his wife, Parul, who is deeply involved in philanthropic endeavors. Their children pursue their academic endeavors in prestigious universities in the United States. Adding to the family dynamic is Rio, the beloved golden retriever, who brings joy and companionship to their home.

Inspired by icons like Warren Buffett and Sachin Tendulkar, Mr. Kohli embodies the principles of wisdom, perseverance, and excellence in both his personal and professional life. His journey serves as a testament to the power of vision, dedication, and integrity in achieving success and making a meaningful impact in the world of wealth management.

Introduction

Family offices are now a fundamental part of wealth management, blending traditional values with modern strategies to address the unique needs of affluent families. Family offices are adopting modern approaches such as comprehensive financial planning, diversified investments, and succession planning to safeguard and grow wealth. The integration of technology, like advanced analytics and digital platforms, is enhancing decision-making and operational efficiency. Additionally, the focus on personalized and ethical investing allows family offices to align financial goals with the values of the families they serve. As these strategies adapt to global economic changes, staying flexible and well-informed is essential for navigating the complexities of wealth management and leveraging opportunities effectively.

Client-Centric Approach in Wealth Management

In the Indian context, a client-centric approach in wealth management is essential for building long-term, trust-based relationships with clients. This approach prioritizes understanding each client's unique financial goals, risk tolerance, and life circumstances. By actively listening and tailoring services to meet individual needs, wealth managers can offer personalized solutions that resonate with their clients. This not only fosters loyalty but also enhances client satisfaction. As India's middle class grows and more individuals seek professional financial advice, wealth managers must shift from product-centric to client-centric strategies. This involves being transparent about fees, risks, and investment rationale and remaining flexible to adapt to changing financial situations and market conditions. Ultimately, a client-centric approach helps wealth managers differentiate themselves in a competitive market and build enduring relationships that drive mutual success.

Vikaas M Sachdeva: What was your initial concept when you started Client Associates in 2002, and what prompted you to embark on that journey?

Himanshu Kohli: When we founded Client Associates in 2002, our vision was to provide comprehensive solutions across a client's balance sheet. Inspired by historical practices like the Munshi in Indian royal families and the emergence of family offices in the West, we aimed to focus on both preserving and growing our client's wealth beyond their businesses. Despite our experience with reputable institutions, we felt the need to prioritize the client's needs over product sales. Hence, we took the entrepreneurial route to establish a client-centric advisory firm, which became Client Associates. Our approach was akin to being a private CFO, addressing all aspects of a client's financial outlook, including financial assets, physical assets, and succession planning. We launched with the goal of providing value-added services beyond what larger institutions could offer, pioneering the family office concept in India. Today, with the dedication of our team and support from partners like yours, we've become the largest multi-family office in the country.

Client-First Principle

The client-first principle is one of the pillars of effective financial services, emphasizing the importance of prioritizing the client's best interests above all else. In India, this principle is gaining traction as more investors seek trustworthy and transparent financial advice. By putting clients' needs at the forefront, financial advisors can build stronger, more meaningful relationships. This involves understanding clients' financial goals, risk tolerance, and personal circumstances and then providing tailored advice and solutions that align with these factors. Adopting a client-first approach also means being transparent about fees and potential conflicts of interest, ensuring that clients feel confident and secure in their financial decisions. Ultimately, this principle helps build trust and loyalty, which are essential for long-term success in the financial industry.

Vikaas M Sachdeva: You once summarized Client Associates' distinctiveness as always being on the client's side of the table. Could you elaborate on that further?

Himanshu Kohli: When I mentioned that Client Associates always sit on the client's side of the table, I meant that our approach is fundamentally centered around the client's perspective. It's not just a matter of convenience; it's a core principle that guides every aspect of our work. This means that our strategies, decisions, and actions are all geared toward serving the best interests of our clients. Instead of pushing products or services onto them, we take the time to truly understand their unique needs, challenges, and goals.

Our goal is to provide tailored solutions that address their specific circumstances and help them achieve their financial objectives. This commitment to a client-first approach is not just a slogan; it's deeply ingrained in our identity as Client Associates, where we see ourselves as partners in our clients' financial journeys, working alongside them to navigate their entire financial outlook and secure their financial well-being. We function as their associates, supporting them across their entire financial outlook.

Adapting to Changing Times

Adapting to changing times is essential for both businesses and individuals, especially in a rapidly developing country like India. The past few years have seen significant shifts in technology, consumer behavior, and market dynamics. Companies that have embraced digital transformation, such as adopting e-commerce platforms and leveraging data analytics, have managed to stay ahead of the curve. Similarly, individuals who have upskilled and adapted to new ways of working, like remote and hybrid models, have found greater opportunities. The COVID-19 pandemic underscored the importance of flexibility and resilience, prompting many to rethink traditional approaches and innovate. As India continues to grow and change, the ability to adapt will remain a key determinant of success, ensuring that businesses and individuals can thrive in an ever-evolving environment.

Vikaas M Sachdeva: As a pioneer in the industry, how has Client Associates adapted to stay ahead of the competition and respond to changing times?

Himanshu Kohli: Client Associates' journey as a pioneer in the industry has been marked by continuous evolution and adaptation to changing dynamics. To stay ahead of the competition, we have consistently embraced innovation and agility. Our proactive approach has led us to introduce groundbreaking services such as trusted advisory solutions, family office structures, and real estate advisory services.

Understanding the significance of illiquid assets in our client's portfolios, we have expanded our offerings to include investment banking services and alternative investments like unlisted funds. By broadening our scope to encompass the entirety of our clients' financial outlook, we aim to secure their trust and capture their complete mindshare, ensuring that we remain at the forefront of the industry's changes.

Family Office Management Styles

Family office management styles in India have evolved significantly, reflecting the diverse needs of ultra-high-net-worth families. There are two primary types: single-family offices (SFOs) and multi-family offices (MFOs). SFOs cater exclusively to one family's financial and personal needs, providing bespoke services such as investment management, estate planning, and lifestyle management. MFOs, on the other hand, serve multiple families, leveraging economies of scale to offer a more cost-effective solution. Indian family offices are increasingly focusing on diversifying investments across asset classes, including real estate, public equity, and startups, while also exploring global opportunities to mitigate currency risk. They are also adopting advanced technologies like AI and data analytics to enhance decision-making and operational efficiency. This shift towards comprehensive, tech-enabled, and globally diversified strategies underscores the growing sophistication of family office management in India.

Vikaas M Sachdeva: Now, moving on to the topic of family offices, can you share your experiences with Indian family offices? Do they tend to be more hands-on or hands-off in managing their investments?

Himanshu Kohli: In discussing Indian family offices, it's essential to recognize the diversity of their approaches to investment management. While some family offices lean towards a hands-off approach, entrusting investment decisions to professionals, others take a more hands-on approach, involving themselves in daily operations.

Through our interactions, we've observed that family offices adopting a hands-off stance often achieve greater success over the long-term. By prioritizing strategic decision-making over micromanagement, they allow professionals to execute investment strategies efficiently and adapt to market changes effectively. This approach promotes a more strategic and forward-thinking investment mindset, positioning these family offices for sustained success in the ever-changing financial environment.

Key Objectives and Differentiation

The key objectives that differentiate one family office from another in India revolve around their unique focus areas and the specific needs of the families they serve. Some family offices prioritize wealth preservation and intergenerational transfer, ensuring that the family's assets are protected and smoothly passed down to future generations. Others may emphasize investment growth, seeking higher returns through diversified portfolios that include equities, real estate, and startups. Philanthropy is another distinguishing objective, with some family offices dedicating significant resources to charitable activities and social impact projects. Additionally, the level of personalized services offered, such as lifestyle management and concierge services, can vary widely, reflecting the individual preferences of the family. Finally, the choice between a single-family office (SFO) and a multi-family office (MFO) also plays a role, with SFOs providing highly tailored services to one family, while MFOs offer a broader but less personalized range of services to multiple families. These objectives and approaches highlight the diverse strategies family offices in India adopt to meet the unique needs of their clients.

Vikaas M Sachdeva: Given the diversity among family offices, what key objectives differentiate one family office from another?

Himanshu Kohli: Indeed, each family office operates within a distinct context shaped by factors such as risk tolerance, family dynamics, and investment priorities. While some family offices may place a premium on succession planning, viewing it as integral to securing the future of their legacy, others may prioritize maximizing returns or preserving wealth across generations.

At Client Associates, we recognize and respect these differences, understanding that our role is to customize our services to align with each family's unique aspirations and circumstances. By tailoring our approach to meet their specific needs and goals, we empower families to navigate the complexities of wealth management with confidence and clarity.

Relocation Considerations for Family Offices

Relocation considerations for family offices in India are driven by several key factors. One major driver is the regulatory environment, as family offices seek jurisdictions with favorable legal frameworks that ensure compliance and protect investments. Tax efficiency is another critical factor, with families looking to optimize their tax liabilities through strategic relocation. The availability of skilled talent and advanced technological infrastructure also plays a significant role, as family offices require specialized expertise and robust systems to manage complex financial operations. Additionally, geopolitical stability and quality of life in the new location are important, as they impact both the operational efficiency and the well-being of the family members and staff. Lastly, the need for better connectivity to global markets and investment opportunities can prompt family offices to consider relocating to financial hubs that offer greater access and networking potential. These factors collectively influence the decision-making process, ensuring that the chosen location aligns with the family office's strategic objectives and operational needs.

Vikaas M Sachdeva: There's been a lot of talk about family offices considering relocation outside the country. What factors are driving these conversations, in your opinion?

Himanshu Kohli: Globalization, coupled with advancements in technology, has made it easier for families to conduct business from anywhere in the world. Factors such as quality of life, business environment, and diversification opportunities are prompting some families to consider relocation. Additionally, recent events like the pandemic have accelerated this trend, with families seeking greater flexibility and resilience in their arrangements.

Real Estate vs. Financial Assets

When comparing real estate to financial assets, each has its distinct advantages and considerations. Real estate investments offer tangible assets that can provide steady rental income and potential for capital appreciation, making them a popular choice for long-term wealth preservation. They also serve as a hedge against inflation and can be less volatile than financial markets. On the other hand, financial assets like stocks, bonds, and mutual funds offer greater liquidity and diversification. They allow investors to spread risk across various sectors and geographies, and they can be more easily bought and sold to respond to market conditions. While real estate requires significant capital and involves higher transaction costs and maintenance, financial assets generally have lower entry points and can be managed with greater flexibility. Ultimately, the choice between real estate and financial assets depends on the investor's risk tolerance, investment horizon, and financial goals, with many opting for a balanced approach that includes both maximizing returns and minimizing risks.

Vikaas M Sachdeva: The allure of real estate as a safe haven for investment is widely recognized. Do you find family offices still gravitating towards real estate, or are they diversifying into other asset classes?

Himanshu Kohli: While real estate continues to be a popular investment choice, we're witnessing a shift toward financial assets among family offices. Factors like the financialization of savings and the potential for higher returns are driving this trend. While real estate remains an essential component of many portfolios, families are increasingly diversifying into a broader range of asset classes to optimize returns and manage risk effectively.

Advisors' Attributes for Family Offices

The attributes of advisors for family offices are crucial in ensuring effective wealth management and meeting the unique needs of ultra-high-net-worth families. Key attributes include a strong educational background in finance, accounting, or related fields, which provides the technical expertise needed for complex financial planning and investment management. Advisors must also possess excellent interpersonal skills to build trust and maintain long-term relationships with family members. An understanding of regulatory and tax environments is essential to navigate the complexities of compliance and optimize tax strategies. Additionally, advisors should have a deep knowledge of both local and global markets to provide diversified investment opportunities. Cultural sensitivity and the ability to align with the family's values and goals are also important, as these factors play a significant role in wealth preservation and intergenerational transfer. Ultimately, the right advisor combines technical proficiency with a personalized approach to cater to the multifaceted needs of family offices.

Vikaas M Sachdeva: What do family offices ideally look for in advisors? Could you give us insight into what makes them very comfortable and convinced?

Himanshu Kohli: Family offices typically look for a few key attributes in advisors. Firstly, they seek control over their complete affairs, aiming for a consolidated view of their overall asset allocation to gain a better grip over their holdings across different entities or asset classes. Consolidation gives them control. Secondly, confidentiality is crucial. They want their information to remain private and confidential. Thirdly, continuity matters. They want to know if advisors are in it for the long-term, focusing on compounding benefits rather than short-term gains.

These three Cs—control, confidentiality, and continuity—provide comfort to family offices. Additionally, trust is vital. They need to trust their financial advisor and seek unbiased advice that prioritizes their interests. Qualifications, track record, and stability of the advisor also matter. Clients want personalized yet knowledgeable service, which is why boutique firms with customized approaches are often preferred. Ultimately, it's about knowing your advisor and their commitment to putting the client first.

Advising Family Offices: Metrics and Insights

Advising family offices in India involves a strategic focus on asset allocation across various asset classes to meet specific financial goals and risk tolerances. Typically, family offices diversify their investments into equities, fixed income, private equity, real estate, and alternative assets like hedge funds and private credit. On average, about 45% of the portfolio is allocated to alternative investments, including private equity and real estate, reflecting a preference for long-term growth and stability. Ideal ticket sizes for investments can vary, but for private market investments, a minimum of $10 million is often recommended to ensure meaningful participation and returns. Family offices generally aim to invest around 5-10% of their Assets Under Management (AUM) in any single asset class to maintain diversification and manage risk effectively. This balanced approach helps family offices navigate market volatility while striving for optimal returns.

Arjun Nagarajan: When advising family offices, what are the key metrics you would look at before advising the ideal product mix? Could you share insights on the number of asset classes or products typically recommended, along with ideal ticket sizes and the percentage of AUM they're willing to invest?

Himanshu Kohli: Certainly, advising family offices involves a personalized approach, considering factors like their risk profile and objectives. We segment the market into various wealth brackets, ranging from retail to ultra-high-net-worth clients. For each family, we assess their risk appetite, growth objectives, and diversification needs. Strategic asset allocation and model portfolios are then tailored accordingly. While there's no one-size-fits-all approach, clients may have exposure to multiple asset classes with diversified managers or products. The ideal ticket sizes and allocation percentages vary based on the family's wealth and preferences. Over-diversification is a risk to avoid, ensuring investments remain meaningful and aligned with their goals.

GIFT City: A Diversification Opportunity

Advising Indian and global family offices about GIFT City involves highlighting its unique benefits as a diversification opportunity. GIFT City, India's first International Financial Services Center (IFSC), offers a range of advantages, including significant tax incentives, a liberal regulatory environment, and state-of-the-art infrastructure. Family offices can set up Family Investment Funds (FIFs) in GIFT City, which allows them to pool resources, invest in a variety of asset classes, and leverage affordable foreign currency loans from local banks. With a minimum corpus requirement of $10 million within three years, FIFs in GIFT City benefit from a 100% income tax exemption for ten consecutive years out of fifteen and no GST on services received. This makes GIFT City an attractive alternative to traditional financial hubs like Dubai and Singapore, offering a cost-effective and strategically advantageous location for managing and growing family wealth.

Arjun Nagarajan: Moving on to another topic, there's been a lot of talk about GIFT City lately. What's your view on advising Indian and global family offices about GIFT City? How do you see it shaping up?

Himanshu Kohli: GIFT City presents an opportunity for family offices to diversify beyond India, mitigating risk while leveraging the liberalized remittance scheme (LRS) and establishing entities for overseas investments. While India remains a promising investment destination, diversification is essential for risk management.

GIFT City facilitates cross-border investments and aligns with the trend of global diversification among family offices. It offers a competitive alternative to established financial centers, attracting interest from industrial houses and family offices. While regulatory clarity and infrastructure development are ongoing concerns, GIFT City has the potential to enhance India's global connectivity and investment ecosystem.

Managing Information Overload

Managing information overload is a key challenge for investors. The constant flow of news, data, and analysis can lead to rushed decisions. To avoid this, it's important to focus on reliable sources and key indicators that fit your investment strategy. Using technology like data analytics tools can simplify the process and highlight what matters. Setting designated times for reviewing updates and staying disciplined in decision-making helps prevent impulsive actions.

Vikaas M Sachdeva: Now, let's talk about the information overload in the market, especially with the rise of social media and the involvement of the younger generation. How do you address the challenge of maintaining a disciplined approach amidst the noise and volatility?

Himanshu Kohli: The abundance of information and social media noise poses challenges for investors, particularly in maintaining discipline and managing emotions. While social media has transformed information dissemination, it also amplifies market noise and short-term biases. Discipline is crucial in avoiding knee-jerk reactions driven by market sentiment. Investors should focus on long-term strategies, asset allocation, and risk management rather than succumbing to short-term fluctuations.

Experience and wisdom play key roles in navigating volatile markets, emphasizing the importance of a disciplined, long-term approach to wealth management. Ultimately, investors must filter out the noise, adhere to their investment principles, and prioritize their financial goals over market noise.

Cryptocurrency in Family Offices

Family offices in India and globally are increasingly considering cryptocurrency as part of their investment strategies. According to recent surveys, about 39% of family offices are either actively investing in or exploring cryptocurrencies. This interest is driven by the desire to stay current with emerging investment trends, the potential for high returns, and the influence of younger, tech-savvy family members. Typically, family offices allocate around 5% of their portfolios to digital assets, balancing the high-risk nature of cryptocurrencies with the potential for significant gains. However, challenges such as regulatory uncertainty, cybersecurity threats, and high volatility remain significant concerns. Despite these hurdles, the growing acceptance of digital assets and the introduction of cryptocurrency ETFs are making it easier for family offices to include cryptocurrencies in their diversified portfolios.

Vikaas M Sachdeva: Let's address a question from our audience about cryptocurrency. What's your view on including cryptocurrency as part of asset allocation for family offices?

Himanshu Kohli: Cryptocurrency represents a volatile yet potentially rewarding asset class. While it has delivered impressive returns over the past decade, regulatory uncertainty and lack of fundamental analysis pose significant risks. Family offices should approach cryptocurrency cautiously, considering its speculative nature and lack of regulatory oversight.

Investing in cryptocurrency should align with the family's risk tolerance and long-term investment objectives. It's essential to conduct thorough research, consult with financial advisors, and limit exposure to an amount that won't jeopardize their financial well-being. As the regulations evolve and market maturity improves, cryptocurrency may offer opportunities for diversification, but prudence and careful consideration are paramount.

Key Takeaways

- **Client-First Principle:** A client-centric approach remains fundamental in wealth management, focusing on deeply understanding and addressing the unique financial goals and circumstances of each client, which builds trust and long-term relationships.

- **Commitment to Innovation:** Family offices that continuously evolve their services and remain agile are better positioned to stay ahead of the competition and adapt to changing market conditions, ensuring they meet the complex needs of modern affluent families.

- **Investment Management Styles:** Family offices that adopt a hands-off investment approach, allowing professionals to manage day-to-day decisions, tend to achieve better long-term outcomes. This strategy emphasizes strategic decision-making over micromanagement.

- **Considerations for Relocation:** Factors like globalization, tax efficiency, and the desire for a better quality of life drive family offices to consider relocating to jurisdictions that align with their strategic objectives and operational needs.

- **Diversification Strategies:** The trend is shifting from traditional real estate investments towards a more diversified approach that includes financial assets like equities and alternative investments, aiming to optimize returns and better manage risk.

- **Attributes Valued in Advisors:** Family offices prioritize control, confidentiality, and continuity in their advisors. Trust and a deep understanding of the family's values and financial goals are crucial for effective long-term partnerships.

- **Personalized Investment Advice:** Tailoring investment strategies to each family's specific risk profile and objectives is essential for achieving financial goals while managing potential risks effectively.

- **GIFT City as a Strategic Hub:** GIFT City offers a compelling opportunity for family offices seeking to diversify their portfolios globally. Its favorable regulatory environment and tax incentives make it an attractive alternative to other financial hubs.

- **Managing Information Overload:** In an era of constant information, particularly with the rise of social media, maintaining discipline and focusing on long-term investment strategies are crucial to avoiding impulsive decisions driven by market noise.

- **Cautious Approach to Cryptocurrency:** While cryptocurrency presents potential high returns, it also carries significant risks. Family offices should approach this asset class cautiously, aligning investments with their risk tolerance and long-term goals and staying informed about regulatory developments.

Chapter 11

Navigating Business Relationships and Stakeholders[11]

- This chapter explores the methods for aligning stakeholder goals, gaining trust, and maintaining a cohesive business environment. The discussions highlight the importance of empathy, integrity, and strategic leadership in handling the complexities of stakeholders.

- Guest Speaker: Mr. Abhijit Bhave, MD & CEO, Equirus Wealth.

  With an illustrious career spanning over 25 years, Mr. Bhave has held significant roles in leading wealth management ventures globally, including Hochibank, HSBC, ICICI Bank, and Karvy Private Wealth. As the CEO of Fisdom Private Wealth, he spearheaded expansion into emerging markets.

- Speaker: Mr. Arjun G. Nagarajan, Commodities Fund Manager, Chief Economist and Communications Manager, Sundaram Asset Management Company

  Arjun G Nagarajan works at Sundaram Mutual as the Commodities Fund Manager. After spending 3 years in academics, Arjun built a career in the equity market spanning over 12 years, with more than 10 of those years being spent at Sundaram Mutual. Arjun was a part of the NITI Aayog's discussion with economists on topical issues in the recent past.

---

11   This chapter is based on The Alternates Universe episode shot on 25-01-24.

Foreword

I am delighted to be a part of the informative collection called The Alternates Universe. We at Equirus Wealth take pride in our position as pioneers in the financial industry, offering personalized wealth management services to our high-net-worth individual (HNI) clientele. Our path has involved continuous growth and adjustment, consistently aiming to provide top-notch investment advice and fund management.

When I look back on my career path, I have been lucky to be heavily involved in different areas of wealth management. In my experience, I have been involved in positions that require not only handling wealth but also comprehending the various requirements of stakeholders. My main focus at Equirus Wealth has always been to combine traditional wealth management strategies with modern, client-centered approaches in order to provide comprehensive financial solutions. This experience has enabled me to collaborate with highly skilled professionals and develop a deep understanding of the significance of flexibility, foresight, and dedication to achieving excellence. These principles have been the bedrock of my work, leading us to overcome the obstacles of the ever-changing financial environment.

The Alternates Universe series has provided a great opportunity for sharing ideas and delving into the numerous opportunities available in the financial industry. It has united intellectuals and creators, forming a community that flourishes through learning and teamwork. The conversations have been valuable and have greatly influenced current thoughts in our field.

While taking part in the series, I found the emphasis on various investment tactics and the significance of a well-rounded approach to managing wealth to be especially valuable. This focus struck a chord with me, strengthening my conviction that a combination of conventional and non-traditional investments is necessary for achieving well-rounded portfolios.

The series offers great benefits to all individuals engaged in the finance industry. It reveals fresh tactics and enhances comprehension of alternative investments, aiding professionals in grasping the intricacies of modern wealth management. This is particularly important for individuals seeking to expand their investment options and make well-informed choices in a more intricate market setting.

In the future, I am excited to see how upcoming issues of The Alternates Universe will build upon these themes and bring new viewpoints that can continue to enhance our field. I hope season 2 will showcase new trends and innovative techniques for wealth managers to stay ahead of the game.

I encourage readers to dive into this book and discover the abundance of knowledge it provides. The shared insights will surely inspire and educate, leading to the development and progress of our field. I would like to express my sincere gratitude to the Sundaram Alternates team behind 'The Alternates Universe' for giving me the opportunity to participate in this impactful project.

The Person Behind the Professional

Mr. Abhijit Bhave is a multifaceted individual known for his diverse interests and remarkable resilience. With an insatiable appetite for knowledge, he is an avid reader, delving into works ranging from Jeffrey Archer to Marshall Goldsmith. Despite his busy schedule, Mr. Bhave prioritizes personal wellness, diligently aiming to achieve 10,000 steps daily and even embarking on ambitious challenges like completing 26,000 steps on January 26th. Mr. Bhave's commitment to fitness is particularly remarkable given his history of overcoming a degenerative bone disease that once threatened his mobility. During the tumultuous times of the COVID-19 pandemic, Mr. Bhave displayed unwavering positivity and resilience, exemplified by his upbeat demeanor even in the face of adversity. A devoted family man, he finds solace in the company of his wife and their son, with whom he enjoys watching Netflix and indulging in his passion for cricket. Their household is completed by a beloved cocker spaniel, reflecting Mr. Bhave's affection for both family and pets.

Beyond his personal pursuits, Mr. Bhave is deeply involved in various endeavors, including public speaking, motivational lectures, and volunteering for the Art of Living organization. As an alumnus, he also contributes to his alma mater through further learning and lecturing engagements. Known for his sharp wit and infectious sense of humor, Mr. Bhave effortlessly connects with people, earning a reputation as a true "people's person." His colleagues praise his keen memory, result-oriented mindset, and openness to diverse perspectives, making him an invaluable team player. While Mr. Bhave exudes positivity and warmth, he holds firm on certain principles, notably punctuality and professionalism. Overall, Mr. Abhijit Bhave's vibrant personality, resilience, and dedication to personal and professional excellence make him a truly inspiring individual.

Introduction

Managing different stakeholders in a business requires clear communication, empathy, and strategic alignment. To effectively manage these diverse groups, it's important to establish open lines of communication and actively listen to their concerns and feedback. Regular updates and transparent reporting can build trust and keep everyone informed about the company's progress and challenges. Aligning the business objectives with stakeholder interests ensures that decisions benefit the broader ecosystem. For example, engaging employees through meaningful work and growth opportunities can boost morale and productivity while maintaining strong relationships with suppliers. This ensures a reliable supply chain. Ultimately, balancing the needs and expectations of all stakeholders is key to building a cohesive and successful business environment.

Identifying Key Stakeholders

In any business, identifying key stakeholders is essential for success. Stakeholders are individuals or groups that have an interest or stake in the company and can affect or be affected by its operations. Employees are vital as they drive the day-to-day operations and contribute to the company culture. Customers are central as their satisfaction and loyalty directly impact revenue. Suppliers ensure the business has the necessary resources to operate efficiently. Investors provide the financial backing needed for growth and stability. Lastly, the community can influence the business's reputation and social license to operate. Understanding and engaging with these stakeholders helps a business align its strategies with their needs and expectations, ensuring long-term success and sustainability.

Vikaas M Sachdeva: Could you elaborate on who the main stakeholders are in a business and which three stakeholders you consider most significant?

Abhijit Bhave: Certainly, Mr. Sachdeva. In any business, stakeholders encompass both direct and indirect parties, ranging from employees and their families to customers, investors, shareholders, partners, government entities, and the local community. However, when prioritizing, I identify customers, shareholders, and employees as the most important stakeholders. Customers are vital due to their direct interaction with the business, shareholders play a significant role in influencing the company's direction and decisions, and employees are essential for driving the company's operations and delivering value to customers. Therefore, focusing on these three stakeholders is essential for the success and sustainability of the business.

Balancing Stakeholder Interests

Balancing stakeholder interests is a vital aspect of managing a successful business. Each stakeholder group—such as employees, customers, investors, and the community—has its own unique priorities and concerns. Employees may seek job security and a positive work environment, while customers look for quality products and services at fair prices. Investors are often focused on financial returns, and the community might be concerned with the business's environmental and social impact. Effective management involves understanding these diverse needs and finding ways to address them without compromising on the overall goals of the company. This often requires open communication and negotiation, and sometimes, difficult trade-offs are made to ensure that the business remains sustainable and profitable while maintaining good relationships with all stakeholders.

Vikaas M Sachdeva: How do you ensure a win-win situation with all stakeholders while aligning everyone's beliefs with those of the company? Do conflicts arise when attempting to create win-win situations?

Abhijit Bhave: Balancing the interests of various stakeholders can be quite challenging, especially in industries like wealth management, where conflicting priorities may arise. For example, if employees prioritize revenue targets over client interests, it could potentially lead to mis-selling, which goes against the core values of the company. Conflicts often arise when short-term gains clash with long-term sustainability, requiring careful navigation and prioritization. To ensure a win-win situation for all stakeholders while aligning everyone's beliefs with those of the company, I believe in adopting a long-term perspective rather than focusing solely on short-term gains.

One effective strategy is to incentivize employees with company ownership or Employee Stock Ownership Plans (ESOPs). By giving employees a stake in the company's success, we align their interests with the long-term goals of the organization, thereby benefiting both employees and shareholders alike. This approach promotes a sense of shared ownership and commitment among employees, ultimately contributing to overall organizational success.

Employee Loyalty in a Changing Job Market

Employee loyalty in a changing job market is increasingly challenging for businesses to maintain. With more opportunities available and the rise of remote work, employees have greater flexibility and options than ever before. This shift means that companies need to work harder to retain their talent by offering competitive salaries, benefits, and opportunities for professional growth. Additionally, creating a positive work environment and ensuring employees feel valued and recognized for their contributions can significantly enhance loyalty. Open communication and transparency about company goals and performance can also help employees feel more connected to the organization. By addressing these factors, businesses can build a committed workforce even in a job market that is constantly in flux.

Vikaas M Sachdeva: You mentioned the importance of employees, emphasizing an "employee first" approach. However, in today's changing job market, do employees reciprocate this loyalty to organizations?

Abhijit Bhave: In today's ever-changing job market, I understand that employees may have various motivations for switching jobs, ranging from seeking better opportunities to pursuing higher financial rewards. However, I firmly believe that prioritizing employees and creating a positive work environment can significantly enhance loyalty within organizations.

To attract and retain top talent, I advocate prioritizing factors such as cultivating a supportive work culture, maintaining transparency in communication, offering attractive long-term rewards, and upholding integrity in all aspects of operations. By focusing on these aspects, organizations can create an environment where employees feel valued, respected, and motivated to contribute their best, ultimately forming a sense of loyalty and commitment that transcends the transient nature of the job market.

Key Considerations for Employers and Employees

In today's work environment, both employers and employees have several key considerations to keep in mind. For employers, attracting and retaining top talent requires offering competitive compensation, benefits, and opportunities for career advancement. Creating an inclusive and supportive workplace culture is also essential to ensure employee satisfaction and productivity. Employers should prioritize clear communication and provide regular feedback to help employees understand their roles and contributions. On the other hand, employees need to consider their career goals, work-life balance, and the alignment of their values with those of the company. They should seek opportunities for skill development and be proactive in communicating their needs and aspirations to their employers. By addressing these considerations, both parties can work towards a mutually beneficial relationship that supports personal and organizational growth.

Vikaas M Sachdeva: What factors do you believe employees should consider when choosing an employer, and conversely, what soft factors should employers look for in employees?

Abhijit Bhave: When choosing an employer, I believe employees should carefully consider several factors to ensure a fulfilling and rewarding work experience. Key considerations include evaluating the organization's work culture to ensure alignment with personal values and preferences. Transparency in communication and decision-making processes is essential for developing trust and mutual respect within the workplace. Additionally, employees should assess the opportunities for career progression and development offered by the organization, ensuring that their long-term goals align with the company's vision and growth trajectory. Furthermore, corporate integrity and ethical practices should be prioritized to maintain a positive and conducive work environment.

Conversely, employers should focus on identifying soft skills and qualities in potential employees that contribute to a positive workplace culture and overall organizational success. Attitude plays a critical role in determining an individual's ability to collaborate effectively, adapt to challenges, and contribute positively to the team dynamic. Skills and expertise relevant to the job role are essential but should be complemented by positive habits and behaviors that reflect a strong work ethic and professionalism.

Most importantly, employers should prioritize candidates with a demonstrated track record of integrity and adherence to corporate governance principles, as these qualities are indicative of ethical conduct and trustworthiness, which are invaluable assets in any workplace setting.

Aligning Employee and Customer Priorities

Aligning employee and customer priorities is essential for creating a harmonious and effective business environment. Employees who understand and are committed to meeting customer needs can significantly enhance customer satisfaction and loyalty. To achieve this alignment, companies should ensure that employees are well-trained and informed about customer expectations and company goals.

Encouraging open communication between employees and customers can also provide valuable insights into customer preferences and areas for improvement. Moreover, recognizing and rewarding employees for delivering exceptional customer service can motivate them to prioritize customer needs. By aligning these priorities, businesses can create a positive feedback loop where satisfied employees contribute to satisfied customers, ultimately driving business success.

Vikaas M Sachdeva: Given your emphasis on an "employee first" approach, how does this align with a "customer first" strategy, and do you have any additional insights on maintaining this balance?

Abhijit Bhave: Indeed. In wealth management, prioritizing employees' understanding of and commitment to clients' goals can lead to a customer-centric approach. By cultivating a culture of empathy and client-centricity among employees, organizations can naturally promote a customer-first mindset.

The Importance of Trust and Integrity

Trust and integrity are fundamental to building and maintaining successful relationships in both personal and professional settings. In a business context, trust between employees, management, and customers is essential for smooth operations and long-term success. When a company consistently acts with integrity, it establishes a reputation for honesty and reliability, which can attract and retain customers, as well as talented employees. Trust encourages open communication and collaboration, enabling teams to work more effectively together. Furthermore, integrity in decision-making and actions helps prevent ethical issues and builds a culture of accountability. By prioritizing trust and integrity, organizations can create a stable foundation for growth and resilience, even in challenging times.

Arjun Nagarajan: Mr. Bhave, you mentioned earlier about putting the customer first in your approach. Could you elaborate on how trust and integrity play a significant role in this?

Abhijit Bhave: Absolutely, trust and integrity are paramount when it comes to customer relationships. I've been fortunate to learn from various experiences in my career spanning different sectors and organizations. From my interactions with affluent individuals to working in public and private sector organizations, trust has always been foundational. In any stakeholder relationship, whether it's with clients or employees, building trust starts with understanding their goals and priorities. As Dale Carnegie famously said, to build successful relationships, you must first understand the other person's needs and desires. By aligning our actions with the best interests of our customers, we establish trust and integrity, which are essential for long-term success.

Managing Stakeholders Effectively

Effectively managing stakeholders is vital for any organization aiming to achieve its objectives. This involves identifying all relevant stakeholders, understanding their interests and concerns, and maintaining open lines of communication. By actively engaging with stakeholders such as employees, customers, investors, and the community, businesses can anticipate and address potential issues before they escalate. It is important to balance differing priorities and negotiate solutions that satisfy the majority while aligning with the company's goals. Regular feedback and transparency in decision-making processes help build trust and ensure stakeholders feel valued and heard. By managing these relationships thoughtfully, organizations can enhance collaboration, reduce conflicts, and drive sustainable success.

Arjun Nagarajan: Managing stakeholders smoothly is critical in any organization. From your vast experience, what do you consider the most effective approach to keeping everyone satisfied, even though it's challenging?

Abhijit Bhave: Managing stakeholders effectively requires a balanced approach. Drawing from my experiences, I've learned that nurturing win-win relationships is key. Just as in a family where each member's needs are considered, stakeholders in an organization must feel valued and heard. One effective strategy is to address their concerns proactively and align our actions with their goals. For instance, understanding what drives each stakeholder—whether it's investors, employees, or partners—and finding common ground can lead to mutually beneficial outcomes. It's about creating a culture of collaboration and shared success.

The Role of Individuals in Organizational Success

Individuals play a pivotal role in the success of any organization. Each person, from entry-level employees to top executives, contributes unique skills, perspectives, and energy that drive the organization forward. When individuals are motivated and engaged, they are more likely to perform at their best, leading to increased productivity and innovation. Encouraging personal growth and providing opportunities for skill development can enhance individual contributions. Additionally, when employees feel their efforts are recognized and valued, they are more committed to the organization's goals. Effective teamwork and collaboration among individuals can also lead to more creative solutions and better decision-making. Ultimately, the collective efforts of individuals determine the organization's ability to achieve its objectives and maintain a competitive edge.

Arjun Nagarajan: You spoke about the importance of individuals over systems in organizational success. Could you elaborate on this perspective?

Abhijit Bhave: Certainly, while systems are crucial for efficiency, it's ultimately the people within those systems who drive success. I've learned this firsthand from Dr. PJ Nayak, my former chairman at UTI, who emphasized personal responsibility and initiative. Motivation, as he rightly pointed out, is intrinsic, and individuals must take ownership of their actions. I often use the analogy of a solar system, where each individual is like the sun, influencing their surroundings. By nurturing a culture of accountability and empowerment, organizations can harness the potential of their people to overcome challenges and achieve success.

The Four E Framework

The Four E Framework—Experience, Earnings, Ease, and Education— provides a simple approach to enhancing business or personal strategies. By focusing on meaningful interactions, financial growth, simplicity, and continuous learning, this framework helps drive long-term success and satisfaction.

Vikaas M Sachdeva: You've outlined the "Four E Framework" in your approach to customer experience. Could you shed more light on these principles and how they guide your strategies?

Abhijit Bhave: The Four E Framework—Experience, Earnings, Ease, and Education—is integral to our approach to wealth management. Experience refers to delivering exceptional service and value to clients, while Earnings focus on generating sustainable returns for investors. Ease emphasizes the importance of streamlining processes and providing convenience to stakeholders. Lastly, Education highlights the need for continuous learning and empowerment. These principles guide our investment strategies and client interactions, ensuring a comprehensive approach that prioritizes long-term success and client satisfaction.

Effective Leadership

Effective leadership is an important aspect of organizational success, as it sets the tone for the company culture and drives the achievement of goals. Good leaders inspire and motivate their teams by setting clear visions and expectations while also being approachable and supportive. They possess strong communication skills, enabling them to convey ideas clearly and listen to feedback from their team members.

Effective leaders also demonstrate adaptability, making informed decisions in response to changing circumstances and challenges. By recognizing and nurturing individual strengths within their teams, they cultivate an environment where employees feel valued and empowered to contribute their best efforts. Ultimately, strong leadership fosters a sense of trust and collaboration, which is essential for navigating complexities and achieving sustained success.

Vikaas M Sachdeva: Good leadership is essential for organizational success. Can you elaborate on what constitutes effective leadership and share examples of organizations that have excelled in resolving conflicts among stakeholders?

Abhijit Bhave: Effective leadership involves inspiring and empowering others to achieve shared goals. It requires integrity, empathy, and the ability to navigate complex challenges. For example, numerous organizations in the wealth management sector have demonstrated exceptional leadership in resolving conflicts and nurturing collaboration among stakeholders.

However, rather than singling out specific names, I believe any organization that prioritizes customer interests and employee well-being will ultimately thrive. By nurturing a culture of trust and transparency, such organizations can navigate conflicts effectively and drive sustainable growth.

Implications of Upcoming General Elections

The upcoming general elections in India are poised to have significant implications for the country's political and economic future. If the ruling party secured a third term, it could lead to continued emphasis on economic reforms and infrastructure development, which have been central to their agenda. Sectors such as manufacturing, clean energy, and digital infrastructure are likely to benefit from sustained government support and policy continuity. The government's focus on initiatives like "Make in India" and incentives for electric vehicles and solar energy could further stimulate growth in these areas. However, the elections also bring the potential for market volatility, as political transitions can impact policies and regulations. A coalition government might slow down the pace of reforms, affecting investor confidence and economic stability. The outcome will significantly influence India's economic trajectory, affecting everything from job creation to foreign investment.

Vikaas M Sachdeva: The upcoming general elections have implications for various sectors. What are your insights into the potential outcomes and sectors that may benefit from the election results?

Abhijit Bhave: The upcoming general elections undoubtedly carry significance for the economy and different sectors. From an investor's perspective, I believe it's essential to focus on three key factors: the economy, investment selection, and external events.

While election outcomes may influence short-term market movements, long-term success hinges on fundamental factors such as economic growth and corporate earnings. As for sectors, consumer discretionary, automotive, logistics, and large-cap banks and IT companies are poised for growth. However, it's crucial to maintain a diversified portfolio and focus on quality investments for sustainable returns.

Advice for Young Investors

For young investors, building a strong financial foundation early on is essential for long-term success. Start by educating yourself about different investment options, such as stocks, bonds, mutual funds, and real estate, to understand the risks and potential returns associated with each. Diversification is key; spreading investments across various asset classes can help mitigate risk. It's also important to set clear financial goals and develop a plan to achieve them, whether it's saving for retirement, buying a home, or funding education. Take advantage of compound interest by investing consistently, even if it's a small amount, as it can significantly grow your wealth over time. Additionally, consider seeking advice from financial advisors or using investment apps that offer guidance tailored to your needs. Stay informed about market trends and economic factors, but avoid making impulsive decisions based on short-term market fluctuations. Patience and discipline are vital, as successful investing is a long-term endeavor.

Vikaas M Sachdeva: Young investors often face challenges in navigating the markets. What advice would you offer to young investors looking to build their investment portfolios?

Abhijit Bhave: For young investors, starting early and investing consistently is paramount. I encourage them to focus on building a diversified portfolio comprising quality stocks and mutual funds. Additionally, educating oneself about financial markets and setting clear investment goals is crucial. While it's tempting to chase low-priced stocks or penny stocks, it's essential to conduct thorough research and prioritize long-term growth over short-term gains. By adopting a disciplined approach and seeking guidance from experienced professionals, young investors can lay a solid foundation for financial success.

Addressing Employee Attrition

Addressing employee attrition is a significant challenge for many organizations, as high turnover can disrupt operations and increase costs. To effectively manage this issue, companies need to focus on understanding the root causes of attrition and implementing strategies to improve employee retention. This starts with creating a positive work environment where employees feel valued and engaged. Offering competitive salaries and benefits is essential, but so is providing opportunities for career advancement and professional development. Regular feedback and recognition can also boost morale and job satisfaction. Additionally, ensuring a healthy work-life balance and addressing workplace stressors can help reduce burnout and turnover. Conducting exit interviews can provide valuable insights into why employees leave, allowing organizations to make necessary adjustments. By proactively addressing these factors, companies can reduce attrition rates and maintain a stable and committed workforce.

Vikaas M Sachdeva: Employee attrition is a common challenge in organizations. What strategies have you employed to address this issue, and how do you prioritize employee satisfaction?

Abhijit Bhave: Employee attrition can indeed impact organizational performance and morale. At our firm, we prioritize employee satisfaction through various initiatives, including competitive compensation, professional development opportunities, and supportive work culture.

Additionally, we emphasize open communication and feedback to address any concerns proactively. Recognizing and rewarding employee contributions is also crucial for nurturing a sense of belonging and motivation. Ultimately, by investing in our people and creating a conducive work environment, we aim to reduce attrition and cultivate a high-performing team dedicated to our client's success.

Key Takeaways

- **Identifying and Prioritizing Stakeholders:** Effective business management begins with clearly identifying key stakeholders—customers, shareholders, and employees—and understanding their unique roles and influence on the organization. Prioritizing their needs supports balanced decision-making and long-term success.

- **Aligning Stakeholder Interests:** Achieving harmony among diverse stakeholder groups requires a long-term approach. Providing employees with ownership stakes can align their goals with the company's objectives, encouraging a shared sense of purpose.

- **Strengthening Employee Loyalty:** Retaining talent in a competitive job market involves more than just competitive pay. Creating a positive work environment, offering growth opportunities, maintaining transparency, and upholding strong ethical standards are crucial for building employee loyalty.

- **Effective Leadership Principles:** Successful leadership involves inspiring others, addressing complex challenges, and creating a culture of trust and openness. Leaders who focus on these principles are better equipped to guide their teams through business challenges.

- **Advice for Young Investors:** Young investors should focus on starting early, investing consistently, and emphasizing long-term growth. Building a diversified portfolio with quality assets is essential for establishing a strong financial foundation.

Chapter 12

Turning from an Intrapreneur to an Entrepreneur[12]

- This chapter explores the transition from being an intrapreneur within a corporate setup to starting one's own venture, highlighting the challenges and strategies for success.

- Guest Speaker: Mr. Nitin Jain, Founder of Neo Wealth and Asset Management.

  Mr. Nitin brings nearly two decades of invaluable experience as a CEO in wealth management, asset management, and capital markets. His illustrious leadership at Edelweiss Group oversaw the management of over USD 40 million in client assets.

- Speaker: Mr. Hitungshu Debnath, Chief Business Officer, Sundaram Alternate Assets Limited.

  Mr. Debnath brings over three decades of experience spanning mutual funds, alternative assets, wealth management, fintech, TPD, and brokering. He is a Chevening Scholar from the London School of Economics and is a Certified Financial Planner. Hitungshu also holds a Master's Degree in CSR and Sustainability from the University of Vienna, Austria, and a Post Graduate Degree in Digital Transformation from Purdue University.

---

12 This chapter is based on The Alternates Universe episode shot on 22-03-23.

Foreword

Our main goal at Neo Wealth and Asset Management is to provide unbiased advice to our clients with utmost transparency and in a very cost-effective manner. After spending almost two decades in this space, I started Neo with the stated objective to 'Do Good' for all our stakeholders. In the last few years, we have seen a huge rise in wealth in the country, and along with that, the clients' needs have also evolved. While most players in the market were offering similar solutions with very little differentiation, Neo's belief in deep knowledge-based and specialized solutions—rather than a sales-push-led, mass-market strategy—distinguishes it sharply from existing players.

Indian investors, especially the sophisticated and evolved ones, have recognized the importance of diversifying their investments beyond traditional options, and I believe that this trend should continue for the next few decades. The Alternates Universe series is an excellent endeavor that allows thought leaders to come together and share their points of view, helping clients further understand the nuances of alternative investing. One lesson that I like to talk about is the importance of having a clear vision when facing uncertainty. As mentioned in my talk, entering the world of entrepreneurship requires courage and an openness to the unfamiliar while remaining dedicated to your objectives. At Neo, we prioritize adapting and evolving while always considering the client's best interests, making this approach fundamental to my leadership.

The Alternates Universe is a rich source of helpful advice and wisdom for wealth managers, investors, and aspiring entrepreneurs. It questions conventional ideas and motivates audiences to reconsider their tactics and methods. The program underscores the importance of having a solid ethical base and ongoing education to maintain competitiveness. I am excited for the upcoming season of The Alternates Universe. I am especially looking forward to more detailed conversations regarding up-and-coming industries and the influence of new technologies on the investment sector. These subjects are growing in importance and have the potential to provide significant benefits to experts at all levels.

Happy reading!

The Person Behind the Professional

Mr. Nitin Jain is widely recognized as an exemplary leader in the fields of wealth management, asset management, and capital markets, boasting nearly two decades of invaluable experience. As the recipient of the prestigious title "Global Indian of the Year 2021," Mr. Jain has left an indelible mark on the industry. During his tenure at Edelweiss Group, Mr. Jain managed over USD 40 million in client assets, showcasing his leadership and strategic skills. In 2021, Mr. Jain founded Neo Wealth and Asset Management, championing trust and transparency in entrepreneurship. Under his visionary guidance, Neo emerged as one of India's fastest-growing investment firms, with assets under advisory totaling USD 3 million. Mr. Jain's commitment to excellence has been further affirmed by the securing of a USD 35 million equity investment from esteemed partners, solidifying Neo's position as a formidable player in the industry.

Beyond his professional achievements, Mr. Jain is admired for his exemplary personal qualities. Colleagues and associates often describe him as patient and affable, possessing a rare ability to connect with people effortlessly. His management style, characterized by empowerment and a focus on learning, has earned him widespread admiration and respect within the industry. Moreover, Mr. Jain's dedication to his craft is matched only by his commitment to his family. A loving husband and devoted father to two sons, he exemplifies the values of integrity, humility, and respect for elders. His deep-rooted passion for literature and cinema further underscores his multifaceted persona, endearing him to colleagues and friends alike.

Introduction

Transitioning from being an intrapreneur within a corporate setup to starting your own venture is an exciting yet challenging journey. As an intrapreneur, you likely have experience innovating and driving projects within the safety net of an established company, which provides a valuable foundation for entrepreneurship. However, stepping out on your own means taking on additional responsibilities, such as securing funding, managing all aspects of the business, and building a customer base from scratch. It's important to conduct thorough market research to validate your business idea and understand your target audience. Building a strong network of mentors, advisors, and peers can provide support and guidance as you navigate the uncertainties of entrepreneurship. Financial planning is also critical, as you need to ensure you have enough resources to sustain your venture during its early stages. Embrace the learning curve and be prepared to adapt and iterate on your business model as you gain insights and experience. With determination and strategic planning, you can successfully transition from an intrapreneur to a thriving entrepreneur.

Transitioning from Corporate to Entrepreneurial Ventures

The transition from being a successful corporate professional to starting one's own venture is often prompted by a combination of personal aspirations and professional motivations. Many individuals are driven by the desire for greater autonomy and the opportunity to bring their own ideas to life without the constraints of corporate bureaucracy. The pursuit of personal fulfillment and the ability to create something unique and meaningful can be powerful motivators. Additionally, some may seek the potential for financial rewards and the satisfaction of building a business from the ground up. The experience gained in a corporate environment, such as strategic thinking, leadership skills, and industry knowledge, can provide a strong foundation for entrepreneurship. Furthermore, changes in personal circumstances or a desire for a more flexible lifestyle can also influence the decision to embark on an entrepreneurial journey. Ultimately, the decision to transition is often fueled by a combination of ambition, passion, and the readiness to take on new challenges.

Vikaas M Sachdeva: You've been an extremely successful entrepreneur, functioning like one even in a corporate setup. What prompted you to transition from being a successful corporate entrepreneur to starting your own venture?

Nitin Jain: It's a decision that's more instinctual than calculated, but my journey with Edelweiss was incredibly empowering. I never felt disconnected from driving the business forward, even as a CEO at a young age. The environment at Edelweiss was conducive to entrepreneurial thinking, with ample support and autonomy. My decision to start my own venture was a combination of logical closure to previous endeavors and a deep conviction in India's future over the next couple of decades. It was about seizing an opportunity to build something fresh with a trusted circle of friends.

Key Differences and Transferable Skills

While both entrepreneurs and CEOs are leaders, their roles differ in scope and focus. Entrepreneurs are typically involved in the creation and initial growth of a business, often wearing multiple hats and handling everything from product development to marketing and finance. They thrive on innovation and risk-taking as they work to establish a new venture. In contrast, CEOs manage established organizations, focusing on strategic planning, operational efficiency, and stakeholder management to ensure sustainable growth. Despite these differences, many skills are transferable between the two roles. Both require strong leadership, decision-making, and problem-solving abilities. An entrepreneur's experience with innovation and adaptability can be invaluable for a CEO facing market changes or pursuing new opportunities. Similarly, a CEO's skills in strategic planning and organizational management can benefit an entrepreneur looking to scale their business. Effective communication and the ability to inspire and motivate teams are also essential in both roles, facilitating the transfer of skills from one to the other.

Vikaas M Sachdeva: It sounds like a smooth transition, but what do you think are the key differences between being an entrepreneur and a CEO, and how do the skills from one role transfer to the other?

Nitin Jain: Interestingly, the core skills required are quite similar, whether you're leading within a corporate or starting your own venture. Team management, strategic thinking, and risk management are all transferable. In fact, running a large firm within a corporate structure can be even more complex due to increased stakeholders. However, there are unique challenges as an entrepreneur, like dealing with mundane tasks such as licenses and office management, which can be overwhelming initially. But, the experience gained from corporate roles definitely helps navigate these challenges effectively.

Building a Strong Team

Building a strong team for your own venture is a critical step towards achieving business success. It starts with clearly defining the roles and skills needed to support your business goals. When recruiting, look for individuals with the necessary expertise who also share your vision and values. Diversity in skills and perspectives can enhance creativity and problem-solving within the team. Once assembled, fostering an inclusive and collaborative culture is essential to encourage open communication and trust among team members. Providing opportunities for professional growth and recognizing individual contributions can boost morale and motivation. Regular team meetings and feedback sessions can help align efforts and ensure everyone is working towards common objectives. By investing time and resources in building and nurturing your team, you create a solid foundation that can drive your venture forward.

Mr. Hitungshu Debnath: You've managed to assemble an impressive team in a short span of time. Could you shed some light on how you achieved this feat?

Nitin Jain: Building a strong team boils down to competence, character, and purpose. Knowing industry stalwarts and understanding their motivations was instrumental in attracting top talent. However, beyond compensation and career growth, people seek purpose. Our firm's purpose of solving complex problems in financial services resonated with professionals seeking meaningful work. Additionally, ensuring a fair and empowering work culture played a significant role in attracting talent. The result is a team of over 700 individuals, mostly hired without consultants, driven by a shared purpose and mutual respect.

Compliance, Risk Management, and Administration

Compliance, risk management, and administration are integral components of a well-functioning organization. Compliance involves adhering to laws, regulations, and internal policies, ensuring that the company operates within legal and ethical boundaries. This not only protects the organization from legal penalties but also enhances its reputation and trustworthiness. Risk management is the process of identifying, assessing, and mitigating potential risks that could impact the organization's objectives. By proactively managing risks, companies can minimize potential disruptions and financial losses. Administration encompasses the day-to-day operations and management of resources, ensuring that the organization runs efficiently and effectively. It involves coordinating activities, managing information, and supporting the strategic goals of the business. Together, these functions help create a stable and secure environment, enabling the organization to focus on growth and innovation.

Mr. Hitungshu Debnath: Your business model at Neo seems to be pioneering. How has your approach to compliance, risk management, and administration changed as a promoter compared to your previous role as a CEO?

Nitin Jain: As a promoter, the accountability for compliance and risk management falls squarely on my shoulders. While the approach remains diligent, there's an added sense of responsibility and scrutiny. I find myself dedicating more time to these aspects than before, ensuring meticulous adherence to regulations. However, my approach to managing people remains consistent. I prioritize open communication, regular interaction, and a supportive work environment, much like I did as a CEO. The difference lies in the heightened awareness of every aspect of the business's functioning, from security to employee well-being, inherent in the promoter role.

Vikaas M Sachdeva: How did the whole journey happen?

Nitin Jain: Well, the journey began with a recognition of key problems within the financial services industry, particularly in advisory and wealth management. When we started, there was no clear structure in place. We identified several significant challenges, one of which was the prevalence of conflicts of interest within the industry due to legacy reasons. We saw an opportunity to establish a transparent and unbiased advisory platform, addressing conflicts by incentivizing our team based on client feedback rather than revenue targets. For instance, in our multi-family office structures, we deliberately avoid revenue targets for our relationship managers to ensure their focus remains on client satisfaction rather than sales figures. This commitment to transparency and client-centricity was foundational to our journey.

Additionally, we observed a shortage of talent, particularly in private banking, which posed a challenge in delivering high-quality advisory services. Recognizing the expertise and experience gap, we sought to create a platform that attracted and retained top talent by offering comprehensive support and resources. By providing seasoned relationship managers with access to our platform's infrastructure and resources, we aimed to empower them to build their practice successfully.

Furthermore, we identified a need for innovative solutions in income generation for affluent individuals. Traditional investment approaches focused solely on capital growth, overlooking the demand for consistent income streams. We endeavored to address this gap by pushing the boundaries of income generation and offering higher yields through strategic asset management strategies. By reimagining the income bucket within wealth management, we aimed to provide clients with financial freedom and peace of mind.

The Incentive Conundrum

The incentive conundrum in the financial services industry, particularly concerning relationship managers (RMs), arises from the misalignment between compensation structures and performance metrics. RMs are often rewarded based on short-term sales targets and revenue generation, which can lead to a focus on immediate gains rather than building long-term customer relationships. This discrepancy can undermine the effectiveness of relationship banking, where customer satisfaction, retention, and loyalty are critical metrics. To address this issue, financial institutions need to develop balanced incentive systems that reward RMs for both quantitative achievements, like revenue per customer, and qualitative outcomes, such as customer satisfaction and retention rates. By aligning incentives with the broader goals of relationship banking, firms can encourage RMs to prioritize sustainable growth and customer-centric strategies, ultimately benefiting both the institution and its clients.

Vikaas M Sachdeva: Can you elaborate on the incentive conundrum you mentioned?

Nitin Jain: Certainly, the incentive conundrum in the financial services industry revolves around the discrepancy between compensation structures and performance metrics for relationship managers (RMs). Traditionally, RMs have been incentivized based on revenue generation, leading to a skewed reward system where even unsuccessful RMs may receive higher compensation than their successful counterparts. This imbalance not only undermines meritocracy but also perpetuates a culture focused on short-term sales targets rather than long-term client relationships.

To address this issue, we reimagined the incentive structure within our organization. Instead of tying compensation directly to revenue, we prioritize client satisfaction metrics, such as Net Promoter Scores (NPS). By incentivizing RMs based on client feedback and relationship quality rather than sales figures, we foster a culture centered on delivering value and building trust. This approach not only aligns incentives with our values of transparency and client-centricity but also ensures that RMs are motivated to prioritize long-term client satisfaction over short-term gains.

Furthermore, we empower RMs to focus on comprehensive client solutions rather than product sales quotas. By providing a supportive platform with extensive resources and infrastructure, we enable RMs to focus on delivering tailored advisory services suited to each client's unique needs. This shift from transactional sales to relationship-driven advisory not only enhances client outcomes but also fosters a culture of collaboration and excellence within our organization.

Transformative Changes in the Financial Sector

The financial sector is undergoing transformative changes driven by technological advancements, regulatory shifts, and changing consumer expectations. Innovations such as blockchain, artificial intelligence, and fintech solutions are revolutionizing how financial services are delivered, offering greater efficiency, transparency, and personalization. These technologies enable faster transactions, improved risk management, and enhanced customer experiences.

Meanwhile, regulatory changes are prompting institutions to adopt more robust compliance measures and risk management practices. Additionally, consumers are increasingly demanding digital and mobile banking solutions, pushing traditional banks to innovate and adapt to stay competitive. This transformation is reshaping the financial landscape, creating opportunities for new entrants and challenging established players to rethink their strategies and operations to meet the demands of a digital-first world.

Vikaas M Sachdeva: Reflecting on your extensive experience in the financial industry, what are the three key factors you believe have significantly altered the industry in the past decade?

Nitin Jain: Over the past decade, several factors have reshaped the financial sector, each contributing to transformative shifts in the industry. Firstly, the rising affluence of Indian society has been a profound catalyst for change. As disposable incomes have increased and consumer preferences have shifted, there has been a significant move towards premium services and luxury experiences. This demographic trend, coupled with the emergence of a sizable affluent class, has created new opportunities for wealth management and asset management firms to cater to sophisticated client needs and preferences.

Secondly, government reforms, such as demonetization, have had a notable impact on the financial ecosystem. While controversial and subject to debate, demonetization led to a significant influx of funds into the formal banking sector, thereby bolstering liquidity and capital flows. Moreover, initiatives like the digital stack have revolutionized financial services, making transactions more accessible and convenient for consumers. The digitization of financial services has not only increased financial inclusion but also accelerated the adoption of innovative fintech solutions, reshaping the competitive landscape and driving operational efficiencies.

Lastly, the COVID-19 pandemic has brought about unprecedented changes in consumer behavior and investment patterns. With heightened uncertainty and market volatility, individuals have become more proactive in managing their finances, leading to a surge in retail participation in capital markets. The rapid expansion of online trading platforms and the democratization of investing have made access to financial markets more equitable, empowering retail investors to take control of their investment portfolios. This influx of retail investors has spurred the growth of discount brokerage firms and fueled innovation in digital investment platforms, fundamentally transforming the dynamics of the investment landscape.

Timing of Equity Dilution

Timing equity dilution is a critical decision for companies, particularly startups, as it impacts both financial strategy and control. Equity dilution occurs when a company issues additional shares, which can reduce existing shareholders' ownership percentages. Ideally, companies should consider diluting equity when they need to raise capital for growth opportunities, such as expanding operations, investing in new technology, or entering new markets. Timing is crucial; diluting equity too early might undervalue the company while waiting too long could mean missing strategic opportunities or facing higher capital costs. Companies often aim to raise funds during periods of strong performance or favorable market conditions to maximize valuation and minimize dilution impact. Balancing the need for capital with the desire to maintain control and maximize shareholder value is a complex but essential aspect of strategic financial planning.

Vikaas M Sachdeva: Could you share your perspective on when the right time to dilute equity is?

Nitin Jain: In the realm of financial services, the decision to dilute equity hinges on the overarching goal. If the aim is to build a substantial and stable institution, capital infusion becomes imperative. Clients seek stability in the institutions they invest in, and capital plays a pivotal role in establishing that stability. At our firm, we have a long-term vision of becoming a dominant force in the financial services sector, and for that, capital infusion is indispensable. However, I emphasize the importance of aligning with investors who share our vision and values. The right partners are crucial for long-term success, even if it means diluting ownership early on.

Common Misconceptions about Entrepreneurship

Entrepreneurship is often surrounded by several misconceptions that can mislead aspiring business owners. One common myth is that entrepreneurs are born with a natural talent for business when, in fact, many successful entrepreneurs develop their skills through experience and learning. Another misconception is that entrepreneurship guarantees quick wealth and success; the reality is that building a successful business often involves long hours, hard work, and the willingness to face setbacks and failures. Some people also believe that entrepreneurs work independently, but in truth, collaboration and networking are vital components of entrepreneurial success. Additionally, the idea that a great product or idea is enough to ensure success overlooks the importance of execution, market research, and customer engagement. Understanding these misconceptions can help aspiring entrepreneurs approach their ventures with realistic expectations and a more strategic mindset.

Vikaas M Sachdeva: Moving on to another pertinent question, what are some common misconceptions about entrepreneurship?

Nitin Jain: One common misconception is the notion that entrepreneurship is inherently tougher than being an entrepreneur within a company. Both roles present unique challenges, but entrepreneurship offers the advantage of driving decisions without bureaucratic hurdles. Additionally, there's a misconception regarding the earning potential of entrepreneurs. Contrary to popular belief, entrepreneurs can indeed achieve significant financial success, as evidenced by various successful ventures in India. Moreover, entrepreneurship offers enriching learning experiences beyond mere monetary gains, contributing to one's personal and professional growth.

Challenges and Advantages for Female Entrepreneurs

Female entrepreneurs face a unique set of challenges and advantages as they navigate the business world. One significant challenge is the persistent gender bias and stereotypes that can lead to difficulties in securing funding and gaining credibility in certain industries. Additionally, balancing work and personal life responsibilities can be more pronounced for women, particularly in societies with traditional gender roles. Despite these challenges, female entrepreneurs often bring distinct advantages to their ventures. They tend to excel in building strong relationships and networks, which are crucial for business growth and collaboration. Women also often bring diverse perspectives and innovative approaches to problem-solving, which can lead to unique business solutions and opportunities. As more women enter the entrepreneurial space, they are paving the way for greater diversity and inclusion in the business world, inspiring future generations of female leaders.

Vikaas M Sachdeva: Insightful observations, Nitin. Now, let's address a question from our audience regarding the journey of female entrepreneurs. How do you perceive the challenges and advantages faced by women embarking on entrepreneurial ventures?

Nitin Jain: The journey of a female entrepreneur undoubtedly comes with its share of challenges, particularly balancing domestic and professional responsibilities. However, I believe there are unique advantages as well. Women leaders often possess exceptional emotional intelligence and maturity, fostering better connections with teams and clients. Moreover, their adeptness at time management, honed by juggling multiple roles, is commendable. At our firm, we actively support women in leadership through initiatives like the Athena program aimed at nurturing future female CEOs. Ultimately, we're all champions of gender diversity in entrepreneurship and stand ready to support aspiring women entrepreneurs in their journey to success.

Key Takeaways

- **Transitioning from Corporate to Entrepreneurial Roles:** Moving from a corporate intrapreneur role to starting a personal venture involves similar skills, such as strategic thinking and team management, but also presents unique challenges like handling administrative tasks and securing funding independently.

- **Building a Strong Team:** Attracting top talent requires a focus on not only competence but also character and shared purpose. Building a team with these qualities ensures alignment with the company's goals and values.

- **Realigning Incentive Structures:** Shifting incentives towards client satisfaction rather than short-term revenue can help create a culture that values long-term relationships and client trust, ultimately leading to sustained success.

- **Transformative Changes in the Financial Sector:** Significant factors like rising affluence, government reforms, and the impact of the COVID-19 pandemic have reshaped the financial industry, creating new opportunities and challenges for businesses.

- **Supporting Female Entrepreneurs:** Women in entrepreneurship face unique challenges, such as balancing professional and personal responsibilities, but also bring distinct advantages like strong emotional intelligence and time management skills. Supporting female entrepreneurs is essential for promoting diversity and innovation in the business world.

Co Hosts

Mr. Karthik B. Athreya, Head – Fund Strategy (Private Credit)

Karthik Athreya oversees the private credit business at Sundaram Alternates. He has helped build an AUM of close to USD 300 million in private credit over the last 5 years that has invested in 18-20% IRR assets across real estate and mid-market lending in India. The Sundaram credit funds he has helped build are known in the market for credit quality, consistent returns, and capital protection. Prior to Sundaram, Karthik ran over a USD 1 billion investment book for Clearwater in India, a special situations fund which invested across special credit opportunities, structured finance, real estate, and distressed situations.

Aside of fund management and principal investing, Karthik has extensive expertise in investment banking, due diligence, corporate finance and risk management from his earlier experience at Rabobank, E&Y, Arthur Andersen and PricewaterhouseCoopers.

Mr. Madanagopal Ramu, Head - Equities & Fund Manager

Mr. Madanagopal Ramu is Head – Equities and Fund Manager at Sundaram Alternates, with over 18 years of experience in the Indian Financial Markets. He currently manages an Assets Under Management (AUM) of around Rs. 3500 crores and has over 8 years of experience in managing funds. He manages Sundaram India Secular

Opportunities Portfolio (SISOP), Sundaram Emerging Leadership Fund (S.E.L.F.) and Voyager PMS strategies which have won awards conferred by PMS Bazaar during their annual PMS Bazaar's PMS Rankings (FY 21-22). He comes with strong academic qualifications, as a qualified Cost Accountant and a Management degree from BIM Trichy.

Mr. Arjun Nagarajan, Commodities Fund Manager, Chief Economist & Communications Manager – Investments

Arjun G Nagarajan is the Commodities Fund Manager, Chief Economist & Communications Manager - Investments at Sundaram Asset Management Company. With an initial 3 years in academics, Arjun's career in the markets span over 12 years, of which he has spent over 10 years at Sundaram AMC.

Arjun was a part of the NITI Aayog's discussion with economists on topical issues in the recent past. In January 2020, Arjun participated in a pre-budget roundtable consultation with the Honourable Prime Minister of India, to discuss the policy measures for Budget 2020-21. He currently manages Sundaram Multi Asset Allocation Fund.˙

Arjun holds a Bachelor's degree in Commerce, MA in Economics and M.Phil in Economics from the University of Madras. He also holds M.Sc. in Economics and M.Sc. Finance & Investment degrees from the University of Exeter, UK.

Disclaimer

material only. While we endeavour to update on a reasonable basis the information discussed in this material, there may be regulatory, compliance, or other reasons that prevent us from doing so. This document is not for public distribution and has been furnished solely for information and must not be reproduced or redistributed to any other person.